IMAGES OF INAYAT

with
a Profile of the Author

SOPHIA SAINTSBURY-GREEN

IMAGES OF INAYAT

by

Sophia Saintsbury-Green

with
a Profile of the Author

SOPHIA SAINTSBURY-GREEN

by

Suria Rebecca McBride

Sulūk Press
Richmond Virginia

Published by
Sulūk Press, an imprint of
Omega Publications, Inc.
Richmond VA
www.omegapub.com

Cover design by Sandra Lillydahl

This edition is printed on acid-free paper that meets
ANSI standard X39–48.

Saintsbury-Green, Sophia Emily Maud (1866–1939)
Includes introduction, biographical note, works cited,
profile of author by Suria Rebecca McBride
1. Inayat Khan, 1882–1926.
2. Saintsbury-Green, Sophia Emily Maud, 1866–1939.
3. Sufis —Biography

Library of Congress Control Number: 2014945602

Printed and bound in the United States of America
ISBN 978–1-941810057

IMAGES OF INAYAT
by
Sophia Saintsbury-Green

Pir-o-Murshid Hazrat Inayat Khan

Contents

Foreword   1

The Man   3

The Murshid   9

The Saint   19

The Master   26

The Prophet   34

Biography of Hazrat Inayat Khan   51

Sophia Saintsbury-Green   53
    by Suria Rebecca McBride

Foreword

This book is not in any sense a biographical one; it deals neither with the life of the master, nor, except indirectly, with the message he brought to the Western world. In the following pages an attempt has been made to present in a series of pen-pictures the various aspects of his personality, in its marvellous blending of the human and divine, with which the writer had the unspeakable privilege to come into contact—in the hope that by gathering them together under the classifications given below, the gracious beauty of his presence may be preserved for future generations.

Each picture depicts but one aspect of his personality, and when it is said "The Saint does not possess such-and-such an attribute," or "The Master manifests such-and-such power," that particular aspect only is referred to; in the being of Hazrat Inayat Khan the different aspects are blent in one harmonious whole.

Note: The terms *murshid* and *mureed* are, in the Eastern school upon which the Master founded his message, synonymous with those of *master* and *disciple*; for the convenience of readers the Western terms are used.

The Man

It requires perfection in humanity to attain to self-knowledge.

Inayat Khan

The *man*! In our limited human phraseology the term we use for the earth terminal of personality, the part that is embedded in the denseness of earth, around which the clinging tendrils of our affections cluster, and from which the magnetism of life's contacts is sent forth. In this sense the Master was a man, in every relation of life giving and receiving the riches of which it was capable, yet in all "treading softly, as one who walks with God." His home life was, to those whose great privilege it was to be permitted to enter into it, simple, dignified, restrained, ordered for things spiritual rather than temporal.

In days of extreme difficulty and poverty during the war (World War I) the welcome of hospitality was always accorded to the visitor—the meals shared with the Master in his Oriental room, although oft-times it was the last food in the house, and it was difficult for those of his family whose devotion had led them to follow him from India, to know where the next meal was to come from.

Can any who have known it ever forget that welcome? The outstretched hands, and the smile that was in itself a benediction. The figure of the Master, robed sometimes in plain black cassock and girdle, at others in the yellow robe of the Sufis; the still calm of the room in the midst of the London traffic, as if a rampart of prayer and peace had been raised around it invisibly. The hours that were in turn years and flying moments, as his words rent the veils of time and space and flooded the soul of his hearers with the light of the eternal.

Pictures chase one another across the screen of memory, tears that wash the heart free of all but gratitude rise now after many years at the remembrance of his graciousness and our blindness, those of us whom as host at his own table he served with divine humility.

Two such pictures let this pen endeavour to paint. It is evening. The disciple has sat on a low divan facing the Master for many hours, lost in the rhythm of his consciousness, led by him through the untrodden ways.

The sun sinks behind the trees of the London square, the sparrows chirp at the windows and the shadows deepen round the calm majestic form, the beautifully modelled head and brow, the slender hands with their passion of renunciation of self and of blessing for the world.

The Master stirs from out a deep silence, one of his little children comes in and leans against him and half absently he caresses the boy. The meal together is a sacrament, for it is given by his hand; the talk is now of life in the world, of the music of East and West, of rhythm and the Russian ballet, of the poetry of Jelaluddin Rumi and Omar Khayyam. Later he takes his vina and, touching its strings softly, sings his own setting of some of the *Rubaiyat*, his voice not merely beautiful to the ear but full of some unearthly power of searching the heart, seeming to blend its quickened beating with the chords drawn from the vina. Afterwards, the train journey of sixty odd miles, alone, yet companioned by his presence, so that his thoughts were our thoughts, and life was seen temporarily through his eyes. The fellow travellers, usually so ordinary, how deep a sense of love arose in our heart for them, what an intense longing to serve the sinful and the sad! In that heightened consciousness even Nature itself assumed a different aspect: the low horizon lifted, and dull blackened buildings held an inner radiance, like the heart of some smouldering fire. Sometimes for days, at times for hours only, it persisted, this expansion of the little self; and when it faded there was still the remembrance and the great expectation of his further blessing.

Another Picture. One such train journey on a cold winter day, this time with the Master; the great London station is full of yellow fog, the raw air trying even to Western lungs and to an Eastern throat, the sensitive throat of a singer, almost poison. The day a public holiday, the train so crowded that it is with difficulty that the Master and the disciple who is with him can obtain seats. At the moment of starting, a poorly clad woman with a young baby in her arms opens the door of the carriage, which is already full. Objections from several passengers—from the Master the greeting usually given to an expected guest. The baby taken from her and held an instant before being placed in the arms of the pupil, the mother seated in the place he had himself occupied. The low "God bless you" is spoken, and then the corridor for the rest of the journey, taken standing in its cold draught, the while his serenity and calm remain unshaken, as though he were enjoying the latest luxury of travel. As *the man,* other pens than the writer's can paint the Master, for into the more intimate relations of so great a personality it is sacrilege for other eyes to look. For in all things human he was beautiful to look upon, in all actions and gestures harmonized to the situation and demand of the moment. Reverence the feeling he inspired at all times, even in those who came in contact with him merely in the ordinary activities of life. His music was to him alike the expression of the deepest life of his soul and the food of his divine inspiration; and many are the pictures which rise before the eye of memory in which the Master is seen with the vina he so dearly loved. One in particular shows him seated on the grass, in a glade deep in the heart of the New Forest, his vina resting against him while he gently and dreamily draws plaintive and soul-stirring chords from its strings, improvising in the different ragas expressive of the beauty of nature and the joy it awakens in the breast of man. It seems as if the sounds of the summer life of the forest are hushed as the exquisite pathos and beauty of the Master's voice fall upon the quivering air; and all around a silence, tense and expectant of some great event, holds sway. In his own words: "To a fine soul colour appeals; to a still finer soul, sound." In all things beautiful he rejoiced, and all things unbeautiful were redeemed from ugliness by his insight and vision. As *man,* the Master lived in the ordinary human life, making no outward claim to be other than his fellows; but, as the sky in the summer night is constantly illumined by the brilliance of the lightning flashes which play through its depths, so was the human personality of the Master constantly irradiated and shot through with divinity, so that to those who were closest to him it became impossible to separate the human from the divine.

The Murshid

The Murshid is the Physician of the Soul.
                                        Inayat Khan

*The saints on the path—blessed be they—
unanimously declare that it is incumbent upon
the neophyte, after the maturity of his conver-
sion, to seek a teacher...versed in the internal
ailments of the soul and their remedies.*
                        Letters From a Sufi Teacher

The soul! That dim stranger to our Western life!
Of whom, among the teachers and preachers
of orthodox religion, can it be said that he is
"versed in its internal ailments and their remedies"? The body and the mind the Occidental
knows, for them and their culture he grudges
no cost, arguing perhaps that if the rind and
pulp of the fruit be sound the kernel will be
sound also. Such the Western outlook upon
life; the Oriental knows better. To him the
soul is predominant, its birth awaited with an

ardour of expectancy, its prenatal stages even forming the golden thread to link all phases of his afterlife.

In the silent places of nature, in jungle and forest, by village wells and at the tombs of the Saints they are to be found, those bringers to birth of the heavenly babe, the Christ-child sleeping in the heart of man. They stand waiting, wise with all wisdom, tender with a great understanding, patient with the knowledge of the frailty of human hearts. Divine men, masters, murshids—a hundred different names men give them in the East; but each and all have the same meaning and significance in the secret sacred language that the soul understands. "Murshid! Master! Khwaja!—my soul is born; after the long travail of body and mind, it lives and cries for sustenance. I have come to thy holy feet and laid it before them: raise it in thy divine arms and teach it the Way that it must go." Such the prayer of the East; and the answer: acceptance by the murshid. No other human tie is like to this; surrender and acceptance, like the arc of the rainbow rising from out two hearts to meet in the heavens.

It was possibly as *Murshid*, more than in any other way, that many of those who heard him teach or play the vina came to know Hazrat Inayat Khan. Lecturing to large audiences gathered by advertisement never made an appeal to him; nor did this medium of expression serve in giving the subtle and mystical present-ment of his teaching. Seated amid a circle of those who, even in the smallest sense of the term, might be called *seekers after Truth*, the Master would speak slowly and rhythmically; in later years, when his knowledge of English was perfected, each word chosen to give the exact shade of the meaning he desired. In the open if possible, beneath the shade of a tree, his listeners grouped round him; he himself looking at those nearest to him, yet seeing none, his slender hand twisting the rosary he wore; his voice with its varied inflections carrying the words he spoke far beyond the brain to make their impression upon the subtler senses which he knew well how to awaken. No didactic teaching his! No appeal to the emotions, no categorical presentment of *logia*[1] of any sort to the mind. In simple phrases, in parable and legends old as the faiths of the world, he lured his listeners on and out, away from the worn-out grooves of thought and the stereotyped ideas of conventional religion, into a new realm of consciousness, fresh and fragrant as the breath of dawn.

Beneath one tree in particular we saw him sit for many hallowed hours in the zenith of

---

1 *Logia* is a Greek word for divinely inspired speech.

the power of his Message; much of what now forms his literary work was given in this spot; the tree, a young one in the midst of a group of larger ones, gave sufficient shade for him alone, and it was his favorite seat. On the passing of the Master from the body the little tree drooped and died, its life over with its sacred mission.

In all his teaching, in whatever form given, the central theme was God; his opening words when giving a lecture or address are significant of his attitude to the world: "Beloved ones of God"—how often have I seen an audience, still restless and indifferent, settle to half-startled attention as those words, so unusual, so poignantly uttered, made their immediate claim. "Beloved ones of God"—to the Master we were all just that! And because of that, his love for each and all of us was unfailing; his patience was indeed of all things about him most divine; his courtesy perfect, his calm never for a moment disturbed. The writer has been with the Master when he was a guest in homes alike of the wealthy and the poor; in each his demeanour was the same. He was apparently unaware of any difference, and his appreciation of the simplest meal or "the most delicious dish" was equal in degree, though he would sometimes apply the latter epithet to something which his hostess had specially pressed upon him.

His serenity was unclouded through all happenings, however untoward. A picture of one such comes to the writer. It is a bitterly cold night in January, the scene a suburb in a north-country manufacturing town in England. Snow has begun to fall, the meeting at which the Master will speak is at eight o'clock, three miles away in the heart of the city. The disciple speaks of a car, the hostess is amazed. "Oh, no! There is a tram five minutes walk from here, we always go that way." There is no telephone, the hour is too late to allow of finding a vehicle of any kind. The little party starts, the five minutes walk is nearer ten and then, "Oh, dear! We have just missed the tram. I thought our clocks were right! Murshid, what can you think of me?" The gentle, humorous reply, "But it is not *you* who are wrong, it is your clocks! We shall blame *them*!" And then the waiting for a quarter of an hour in the murk and slush and bitter wind, and no word to show that the Master even felt discomfort. He spoke of different things in his even tones; and once his pupil listening had the sudden vivid impression that they stood in a cowslip meadow and that the icy wind was the soft breeze of spring.

Never to blame: that was the Master's basic principle in dealing with his mureeds; always he saw the good in their actions; or, when there was no good to be seen in some particular condition or circumstance, he would picture that condition as absent and dwell upon the opposite virtue. On one occasion someone was telling him of an unusually "bad" action (in the usual acceptance of the term *bad*) and ended by suggesting that to have such a person as the one who had committed it known to be a disciple of his would produce a bad impression upon others. The Master listened attentively to a list of the wrong doings of the aspirant to membership, and then replied with a smile, "Well! and now that you have told me what he has done yesterday we shall ask what is he doing today? Or, still better, what will he be doing tomorrow? Perhaps we shall melt his faults in the fire of our love!"

It was the custom of the Master to give a new name to the neophyte upon his reception as a disciple, and many of the names he gave were suggestive of the particular ideal towards which the character of that individual needed to develop. In the place of severity or displeasure the Master would have recourse to a gentle humour, sometimes holding up to the eyes of the pupil some weakness or failure. In most cases, however, it was sufficient for the devoted disciple to come into the light of his presence; so much did he expand the consciousness, faults and mistakes in the character seeming to rise of themselves and float before the inner vision like motes in the sunshine. Verily he did melt not only faults, but all the knots and cankers into which life warps even in finest natures, in the fire of his love; or, as it would often seem to those about him, in the radiance of his being.

As *Murshid* he was ever unwearied in love, patient with lack of understanding, tolerant of prejudice and ignorance, courteous towards opposition, unruffled by antagonism. At one of his lectures a good deal of interruption was caused by a rough man of the uneducated class who continually called out words of disagreement. The Master, who spoke without a chairman, at last took notice of the disturbance and, after some unusually blatant contradiction, said in his usual even tones: "Yes, perhaps it may be so! But shall we wait a little to discuss it, as these others may like to listen to what I am saying just now?" The man was abashed and sat down. When the lecture was over the Master called him, but as he was too sullen to come to the platform, he himself went down the hall to him. They spoke together for some minutes, and then, to their great astonishment, his disciples saw the man take the hand of the Master and shake it excitedly, while he said in a loud, hearty voice: "Well, sir, I don't know now as I thinks just like what you do! But I'd like you to be my *Friend*." Father! Mother! Friend!—the Murshid is all and more to the devotee who gives himself wholeheartedly to his training.

But like a great surgeon he also knows when to use the knife, and the diseases of the soul need surgery more subtly delicate than any physical organism, however vital or complex it may be. Old growths of prejudice and intolerance, dead tissues of past loves and hates, old psychological conditions and complexes of many and various kinds—all such he knows how to treat, turning upon them the healing rays of his compassion, burning up the waste of the years in the white fire of his love.

No words if they could be avoided; those who were nearest to him learned to wait in the silence for his guidance. "Let us have a silence together" came to be the phrase most eagerly awaited by such; and to the rhythmic waves of the atmosphere that was most truly himself they surrendered themselves as some strong swimmer may relax and abandon himself to the gentle motion of a summer sea. To sink into the still deeps that lie within us all, upheld by the vibrations that pulsed with steady swing at first, and then, as if polarized to that presence, turned in upon themselves to form a shell of silence. To hear the life within at its ceaseless, effortless task of being—to step, at first timorously and clinging to each breath of the Master as a child to its mother's hand and then, with increasing confidence, a little more bravely, back from those busy looms of body and brain and away from the confines of the known; to feel as in a dream the movements of the soul, as one may feel a faint wind stir among the trees at dawn, to bathe in the sources of the Infinite; and, though as in sleep, to feel the Touch upon one's brow—these awed moments were his gift to us, these great renewals heralded by the words, "Shall we have a Silence together?" What pen can paint the closer intimacies of spiritual communion between the soul and the one to whom it gives the sacred name of *Murshid*?

The mystical significance of such a communion must be experienced to be understood; its sacredness must be felt rather than described. A surgeon has told the writer that he once held a living heart in his hands for the fraction of a second and felt it beat. The Murshid holds the living heart of his mureed in his hands; gently, as one might hold a captive bird; for the fraction of a second only he holds it so, when in the first great recognition it leaves the breast of the disciple to lose itself in his being. Then it is given back with his seal upon it, the seal which is the insignia of his divine office and which stamps it, *not* with his own name, but with the name of God.

The Saint

He who fights his nature for his ideal is a Saint; but he who subjects his ideal to his realization of truth is the Master.

Inayat Khan

It is not the solid wood that can become a flute, it is the empty reed.

Inayat Khan

A Saint is one whose past failures have become a life-giving fragrance.

Dar-u-Salaam

By what attributes does the ordinary man recognize Saintship? What is his conception of the meaning of the term? And to what type of his fellow man does he apply the name of *Saint*? Various though the answers to such a question may be, there is surely one point upon which they would be unanimous, one attribute which would appear in the eyes of all thinking men to be essential to the nature and character of Saintship. This attribute, or rather this quality, which is resultant from the absence of most of the other attributes of human nature, is known in our common parlance as *selflessness*.

In those men or women to whom their fellows accord the name of Saint, the absence of that central pivotal factor of human existence, the ego or *I*, is the first and most salient appeal made to the minds of others. The tough fibres of individuality have been pierced, and the interior recesses of character burned away, and from the "empty reed" comes forth the music of Orpheus, divinely compelling, challenging in its unearthly beauty, awakening an inarticulate homesickness in even the most undeveloped lives. The music of the spheres, and the fragrance of healing balsams distilled from herbs gathered by the wayside on the road of life—such are the gifts that distinguish the Saint from other men, whether he be king or beggar, known or unknown to the world at large.

Resentment he has laid aside, and in its place he wears the breast jewel of compassion, clasping the robe of humility about him as he treads the common ways of men. Not his the rapturous vision of the Seer, revealing heights beyond those paths beaten hard by the toiling millions as they go; not for him the ecstasy of the Mystic whose thought is a kindled flame in the central fire of the being of God. The thunders of prophetic utterance are not vouchsafed to him, and for him no burning bush reveals the immanence of God. His ways are the common ways of men, his hands bring to them healing and the surcease of pain; his gentle presence stirs no wonder in their minds, they drink from the chalice of his open heart and pass on refreshed.

The prayers of the Saint are the incense rising from the altars in the shrines of all men's hearts; he keeps alight the lamp of the soul which they are too negligent or ignorant to tend. His feet are wounded with the stones they have left in the gardens of their lives, and his garments soiled with the dust of their incessant haste. The memory of his failures he does not lay from out his heart, for each one has become for him a thorn, and by the miracle of God's grace is changed into the mystic rose, whose fragrance keeps the memory of Eden fresh at the heart of the world. Of all the mysteries of the being of the Master, the disciple who strives to paint these pictures was perhaps most deeply moved and most intensely drawn by the moments that revealed his Saintship. Two such may be given in these pages; others are too intimate in their dealing with the lives of his devotees to be depicted for the outer world.

Again the disciple was travelling with him, and together they had left the home of a member of his followers in which there had been an atmosphere more than usually congenial to his way of life and thought. He had been calmly cheerful when the journey began, looking untired and untroubled, young, buoyant, almost gay. During the journey of an hour he talked with the pupil, discussing a book he was writing and plans for the work at the place to which they were going. Suddenly he broke off in the midst of a sentence and, leaning forward, gazed earnestly from the window at the flying fields, with an expression of deepest pain and sorrow changing every line and muscle of his face; and, as the disciple saw with amazement, his hair becoming grey at the temples.

The plan arranged was not followed when the station was reached, for the Master, scarcely hearing what the disciple said, made a gesture of farewell and moved away among the crowd. The change from a young, upright and manly form was so extraordinary that the pupil stood, dazed and wondering, to watch the bent figure of an old man, bowed beneath some mysterious burden of sorrow as it disappeared from view. No explanation of this unusual occurrence was given then or afterwards, and when the Master took his class a few hours later he had again assumed his normal appearance. Two years later the disciple witnessed a similar change, which took place when the Master was holding a class for his immediate circle of pupils and which was observed by them all. Among themselves they spoke of it when the class was over, and one of them said, "It seemed as if he were torn by some cosmic agony." The hour of the class was three o'clock in the afternoon; at seven the same day telegrams in the evening papers gave the first notices of the great and terrible earthquake in Japan.

One other picture: it is after a lecture given by the Master in a church in a south of England town, and the hour is late. In the vestry for a long time people have been succeeding one another in interviews with him, seeking advice in all kinds of difficulties, spiritual and temporal. At length they are all gone, the old verger has turned out the lights, and only one remaining lamp over the door illumines the church. The disciple awaits the Master in the dim building, alone, as it would seem, when suddenly a movement is felt rather then heard in one of the darkest corners, and two figures move from the shadows. They approach the disciple, who sees that one is that of a woman, and that she leads by the hand a man, whose head and face are covered almost entirely with white wrappings, falling loosely as if just undone.

In broken words the woman speaks: "The great Saint! Last night I heard him speak and this evening I have brought—no! do not look!—but would he, could he help?" It is too late, sick and shuddering the pupil involuntarily recoils: for in that instant it was visible! A face—human once, but now so marred and ravaged by the foulest of all diseases that but half of it remains. So awful is the sight that even its piteousness is powerless to prevent the horror too instinctive to be kept back. The woman draws the merciful folds of the enswathing bandage into place; but all the time she is repeating her half articulate request, "*would* he?—*will* he?—"

Ah, yes, he is there, standing at the door of the vestry and beckoning them in; it closes behind the trailing forms and once more the dim silence enfolds the waiting disciple. They do not again enter the church, but go out by another door, and after a long interval the Master comes. No word is spoken on that homeward walk, but ever and again, with a deep sigh, the Master lifts his head and looks up at the dark blue sky of night, in which there is no light except the stars. And then, as a cry from a heart over-burdened and borne down by the sins of the world, there come all at once the low, intensely uttered words: "I would rather be known as the Great Consoler than as a Great Teacher." Unconscious of any human presence, he walks on in a deeper silence; and the pupil, following, knows that the veil has been for an instant lifted to show the features of a Saint of God.

The Master

Illuminated souls do not seek after occult powers, but occult powers by themselves come to them.

Inayat Khan

Power is the note of the Master, as service that of the Saint; but like the reverse sides of a single coin one is the complement of the other, one hidden while the other is revealed. In Hazrat Inayat Khan the power of the Master was continually felt by his disciples, and manifest at all times as a force underlying his actions and words in the Message; but, in accordance with the occult law which governs all high spiritual development, it was never once used by him for the personal advantage of himself or those related to him by family ties. In the usual bearing of the Master, in his figure, in his carriage and the poise of his head, the consciousness of power was evident; yet it was a power held, as it were, in leash, and strongly controlled by the will, lest, as some strong wind may tear aside a disguising veil and reveal the hidden features within, it might disclose beneath the humility of the Saint, the majesty of the messenger of God.

In all ages, among all peoples, and in every land trodden by their sacred feet, they have been thus veiled, the great masters of the wisdom who have come to bring the light of truth to humankind. For the Message of the age must make its own way into the hearts prepared by faith and divine grace to receive it; imperceptibly it flows in the ordinary channels of men's lives, leaving in its wake a new fertility and richness in the arid soil of their minds. No beating of drums proclaims its advent, no fanfare of trumpets heralds the passing of the one who brings it to the world; a stranger to the seats of the mighty, unknown or ignored by the rulers of the people, he comes, and is once more gone.

In his gift of healing the sick does the Master permit his power the fullest and most untrammeled scope, though even the exercise of this manifestation varies according to the rhythm of life in any particular age and race, and in accordance with the intellectual and physical development of the people of the time. For it is as true in our own day as it was twenty centuries ago, that often "he could do no miracle there because of their unbelief." Yet, where the response of recognition and faith leapt up to meet his presence, the Master would never withhold the healing power that was his, and his compassion was ever at the service of the sinful and the sad.

The disciple who paints these pictures is able to give personal testimony to the great blessing received from the healing of the Master after having suffered from a serious internal complaint which had caused eleven months to be passed in bed. During this time four doctors gave it as their verdict that without an operation no cure was possible, but that the condition of the heart prevented one being attempted. The Master, who was staying near the disciple's house, hearing of the illness, came instantly, and by the bedside gave the healing blessing of the *Laying on of Hands*, an immediate cure resulting and no symptoms of the illness having recurred during the ten years which have passed since that day. A strange phenomenon of the case may be recorded here: during a wakeful night a short time before the visit of the Master the disciple perceived a large circle or disc of white light which seemed to be projected into the room through the wall *behind* the bed, and remained steadily for several minutes suspended in the center of the room, coming from the *opposite* side to that in which was the window. (The disciple had seen a similar circle of light about a year previously when lecturing on the universal expectation of the second Coming of the Christ.)

On the day following this vision, a friend living in the adjoining hotel, came to visit the disciple, who inquired if there was any visitor of an unusual type staying there. The Master was described to her as an Indian philosopher and musician who was, the speaker believed, giving a course of lectures in the town.

In later years the Master was asked by another disciple how it was that the healing in the particular case just recorded had been instantaneous and complete, while in other cases known to the questioner it had not always been so. His reply, "it depends upon the response," is a paraphrase of those other sacred words, "according to your faith be it unto you," and teaches the great truth, on which he was always insisting, that it is *the God within* who heals—the work of the healer, so-called, being like that of a water-finder, to discover the life-giving stream in the depth of man's being, and set free its hidden springs. In some natures the stream is nearer the surface than in others, and the whisper of its waters as they pass over the rocky bed of human character is the voice that men call *faith*. The cure, of which a slight account has been given here, is only one of many that the Master brought to pass in the lives of those about him; but, as has been said in the "Foreword," it is only experiences entirely personal to the writer that these pictures attempt to depict.

A difficult task indeed to turn over the leaves of the book of memory and read upon each page the story of some sacred moment; or to see some picture poignant in its beauty or encircled, as with a garland of little simple flowers, by a thousand instances of kindliness and consideration in the common things of life. And underlying all, his power that, like a drawn sword flashing from the scabbard, would at times leap forth to prove him warrior as well as Saint, Master as well as servant of humanity. To be with him was to dwell upon a veritable Mount of Transfiguration; on which not only he himself, but all scenes and characters about him, became startlingly clear with a transforming quality of *newness*, so that the inner as well as the outer aspects of their being came into view.

The disciple sees another picture, and again the scene is a journey, for during the brief years in which he lived in the Western world, the Master travelled unceasingly, bearing the seed of the Message to the lands in which it must be sown. The journey is from Holland to Paris, and the way taken is through part of the country then known as the *Devastated Area.* The train is approaching Mons, that name which no English heart can hear without the tremor of an anguished pride and pain, that spot sacred through all future generations as the Calvary of an unspoilt youth of a nation.

The Master feels the quickened pulse of the disciple's heart and with his unfailing response to need he answers it. Turning to another pupil, who is not of the English nation, he asks to be left alone with the disciple; and, when the door into the corridor is shut, he looks steadily out of the window for a moment or two, and then closes his eyes. The disciple followed his example; and then, with his power staying and supporting through endless vistas and red-hot mists of agony and pain, sees as it was—the War. No words can paint those scenes—though many pens have tried; seen as it is now by the disciple in one complete whole (and not, as by those who took part in it, in separate sections and fractions of sections), to see the *War* is to see into the cauldron of hell itself—a cauldron from which arise, as from some vast abyss in the bowels of the earth on which we live, the fumes of a poison deadlier than death, brewed from the lusts and hates of men.

Red skies and murky clouds of pitch, the stench of dissolution and decay, the foulness of the tainted air and breath of human life!— all this and more have many seen, and told it in the quiet days of peace; but not to them might it be given to see the picture that God saw and *lived*, lived as we men have marvelled He could do, unmoved and silent while an Age passed out beneath His feet. Not theirs to see the life that leapt immortal from the festering clay, not theirs to note the white souls trooping up to God. The soldiers saw the angel hosts at Mons, for once the enshrouding horror broke and let them through; but only once the glory flamed from out the pit, and all the time those heavenly forms were there, and pain was drenched with dew from out their hearts, and dim eyes glazing saw their light and closed to wake with God.

The vision fades, the curtain closes down; that heavy-hanging pall that shuts men in, hiding the further vision from their eyes. The Master breathes upon the ebbing life that flutters like a stranger in the pupil's breast, and feeds its feebleness with grapes and bread broken and given with his sacred hands. His power has opened wide the prison gates and flung aside the windows of the *known*; and now his great compassion draws them closed lest too much vision burst the bonds of sense.

In many ways, and by small, apparently unconscious acts, the Master gave evidence of the power that was his; one such occurs to the mind of the disciple now. It was unusual for him to speak much when walking; but, on this occasion, he had been sitting for an hour or more in Regent's Park, and on leaving, continued his discourse as he paced slowly, the disciple at his side. On reaching the cross-roads by Baker Street Station, the Master, without pausing or altering for an instant the rhythm of his walk, stepped off the pavement into the stream of traffic. Alarmed for his safety, in spite of faith in all he did, the pupil followed, and with the same slow pacing step they crossed the double lines of swiftly moving vehicles.

Once only the Master raised his hand, and vividly the disciple remembers the words, heard while a plunging dray horse touches with its head the calm, unhurried form: "And I tell you, my *Mureed*, that every thing which has praise from the world is unnoticed in Heaven, and everything which is unnoticed by the world is kept in Heaven." They move on between the wheels and through the maze of human endeavour; and once again it seems to the heart of the pupil that a great silence falls upon the world.

The Prophet

The Prophet is the painter of that ideal which is beyond man's comprehension.

Inayat Khan

There exists in the East a widely different conception of the term *Prophet* to that which is prevalent in the thought of the West. The latter point of view limits the name of *Prophet* to those great characters depicted in the Hebraic scriptures as possessing the power of prophetic utterance; for instance, while Elijah, Elisha, Isaiah, Jeremiah and others are entitled to be called *Prophets*, Jacob, Joseph, Moses and many other great Biblical personalities would not be so designated. In the East, and especially in the teachings of Islam, the name of *Prophet* is the most exalted that can be applied to a divinely inspired human being, and is in fact synonymous with that of *Avatar* in the Hindu terminology: both having the

34

connotation of a blending of the human with the divine at such a high level of consciousness that *union*, or God-realization, has been attained. The phrase, "In the prophetic line," is used to denote one who, in the hierarchical succession of divinely inspired men, comes to the earth with a definite mission and forms part of the chain of those who have been known to past ages as the teachers and saviours of humanity.

In this sense the term is interchangeable with that of the *Messenger*, yet there is a certain difference in its application and significance; for while all those who have brought a message of truth to the world were most certainly also Prophets, all Prophets were not definitely Messengers; that is, they did not bring an explicit restatement of truth, in the form of a religion, to the age in which they lived.

As in the distinction drawn between the Master and the Saint, the note of the former is positive and expressive and that of the latter negative and receptive, so on a higher level still, the Prophet wields the power of God and the Messenger embodies His love. To some minds it may appear presumption or even blasphemy thus to attempt to define and classify characteristics as far above the normal human development as are the snows of the Himalayas from the plains that lie beneath.

Yet, even as a child can feel the subtle distinctions in the characters of his elders, and by observing them grows in wisdom himself, so does the human heart expand and develop by the effort to appreciate the characteristics of high and holy souls, seeing in each aspect one facet of the perfect whole.

In his Prophetic aspect the Master was possibly further removed from those whom he permitted to call themselves his disciples than in any other. At such moments it seemed that he withdrew from the beloved physical form they knew, and in the place of the sunshine of his presence, a chill wind of separation blew between themselves and him. Naturally it was not possible for them to know the nature of the call that came to turn his thoughts away from them, or to summon him to councils held in the secret places of the earth. Only they knew that he was gone; sometimes in the physical body, but more often *from out* the body; while it yet remained with them, swiftly and unaccountably he would be gone, leaving but an automatic rhythm of consciousness behind.

A picture of the former way of going rises to the disciple's memory and may be given here, so far as human words can image happenings not of this world. The scene: a little village on the coast of Holland, then but a collection of fishermen's huts at one end of the beach, and at the other a few hotels, open for summer visitors, but at that season closed and silent. The Master is staying at the house of one of his disciples, and the writer of these memories is also there. The wide windows of the studio in which he taught look west across the grey autumn sea, and, all around, the wastes of sand dunes catch and hold the eye with their suggestion of distance from civilization and its importunate desires.

Peace. Silence. With the ocean awash at its gates, the ordered rhythm that was his atmosphere and in which he tuned the broken human chords to harmony with God—all this and more formed as it were a web of mystery and beauty in which his pupils moved, as in a dream, throughout the tranquil stillness of the fading year. Always his serenity was the setting of their days; his calm, the benison that touched their nights with peace; his humor, like the sun upon the sea, playing with all their passing waves of thought.

And then—a day when, without warning, that most wonderful rhythm trembled upon itself and broke. A strange restlessness took its place, and during breakfast the Master neither spoke nor touched the food upon his plate. The morning passed as usual, but those grouped around him saw that his thoughts were far away. His sentences were left unfinished, his movements showed a restlessness altogether new to them. At lunch, again he neither spoke nor ate; but on rising from the table he asked his host and the disciple who writes to accompany him for a walk. They hasten to fetch their coats, but, quick as they are, his impatience is evident; he is waiting at the door, and, as they appear, walks hurriedly inland toward the wastes of sand.

Faster he walks, with a gait so unlike his measured steps that they glance at one another in surprise; and soon it is only by almost running that they are able to keep close to him as he goes. After some ten minutes walk they reach the dunes, and there the Master stops; imperiously, and in a voice they scarcely know, he bids them wait till he returns, and, awestruck by his manner, they obey in silence.

The spot in which he leaves them is a little mound on which a flagstaff has been fixed; and from it the two who wait can see the Master's figure as he walks rapidly, in long strides, planting his stick before him in the shifting sand. He is bareheaded, and his hair, usually so expressive of his love of beauty, is all dishevelled and streams out upon the wind. His garment, a long black cassock and overcloak, adds to the impression of some

Prophet of old; and involuntarily the disciples utter the same word: "Elijah!" How is it that we *know* he looked like that?

His haste does not impair the sense of majesty and power that comes to them as they watch that figure while it seems to grow larger instead of smaller in the distance, until some quarter of a mile away it disappears among the further dunes. For perhaps three-quarters of an hour they wait in silence which is like a prayer; and then they see him come, not by the path by which he went in urgent haste, but slowly and with measured steps, his aspect of such beauty that they catch their breath.

Gently he treads the narrow sandy way, and as he comes he stoops to gather flowers, the wild and hardy poppies of the sea, the thistle and the yellow spikes of gorse. His form is slender now and full of grace, his hair is smooth upon his brow; he smiles the heavenly smile that wins their hearts, and, bending, lays the flowers in the pupil's hands. He talks of usual matters on the homeward way, and lightly touches each in humorous vein; no word is said, no question asked that can refer to that strange hour; and so, their hearts alight with joy, they reach the house. Only at supper, which is always a sacrament of peace, he speaks of what has passed. His host is asked if he can find the spot, a tiny basin green and fresh with grass, behind the mount near which the Master disappeared. "For from today it shall be given the name *Murad Hassil*, the Mount of Blessing; and those who pray for blessings there shall have their wish granted." So spoke the Master, and no more; but in their hearts the two disciples thought: "It is the place of tryst; he kept it there—with Whom?"

At night it was the custom of the Master to visit a disciple who was lodging near by and suffering much from pain and loss of sleep; after he had done so a few times, his host noticed that the fishermen grouped themselves at the corner by which he was accustomed to pass, and all raised their caps as he went by. Curious to know their feeling, he spoke to one of the elder men and learned that they believed the Master to be St John the Baptist.

Why they chose this particular saint it is hard to say; one would think rather that they might have seen in him the one who called the fishermen of old and walked with his disciples on the Galilean Sea. And yet, it was the first aspect of the Messenger, the *power* of the Message rising and burgeoning within his breast, that marked the Master most during those days beside the sea. And to these simple souls it made its strong appeal: wordless and wonderful, it spoke to them of God.

In quite another setting recognition came to the Master from souls equally simple, yet of a far different type. He had been speaking in the East End of London, and was returning by train from the Whitechapel district. At one of the stations a group of working boys and girls got into the compartment and some noisy argument began among them and soon took the form of a quarrel in which bad language and oaths were the chief feature. The Master remained unmoved and did not attempt any interference; only, after a few moments, he removed the black fez which he always wore when travelling, and which acted as a partial disguise, covering, as it did, the noble upward sweep of the brow. After a minute, a girl of about sixteen looked towards the corner where he sat, and gave a startled cry. Putting her hands over her eyes as if to hide the vision that broke upon her, she shrank back against the lad next to her, saying in a hoarse whisper, as if to herself, "Oh my God! It's Jesus Christ!"

A stillness like death succeeded the clamour of a few minutes before, and was broken only at the station at which the Master was leaving the train. We are told that the type of the savior of humanity always persists, and that the great mediaeval painters have portrayed the Christ from an intuitive recognition attained by the inspiration of their subject. It would seem that it is in our own age, as once before, that much which is hidden from the learned is revealed to the simple and to babes; for, in other instances and in widely differing lands, the recognition of the Master as some embodiment of their ideal of the divine has been instantaneous among those who saw without either an intellectual or spiritual comprehension of the Message or the Messenger. Apart from the action of the brain, and often in spite of the dictates of reason, the soul can see in flashes of vision; but without the concurrence of these sentinels of its prison house it may not do more than glimpse the passing vision, before the shades close in once more. Deeply, profoundly, true are the words of Sri Krishna in the Bhagavad Gita: "The mind is the slayer of the real, O Arjuna; let the disciple slay the slayer."

The Message, what is it? To answer this question does not come within the scope of this little book, these blown leaves from memory's tree, gathered together to form a garland for the sacred shrine of the Messenger. Only, that in the far-flung seed of that Message is the kernel of the spiritual food that shall be for the healing of the nations; only, that in the power of that Message conscious union with God will be the heritage of humanity, realization of his own divinity the ultimate goal of the age-long evolution of Man. Love for *all*, harmony *with* all, beauty *in* all: to experience this trinity of consciousness is the next stage of man's unfoldment of the Spirit that has led him on, upwards from stone to plant, from plant to beast, from beast to man. "Our little systems have their day," but in each the end and aim is the same: the realization of the utmost scope of human development; the realization of the true nature of Man's own being; the realization of *God*. To this end are the Messengers born into the world, that at each stage and at every phase of its upward climb the world may have light, and still more light.

For as light is always one and the same, whether it be made manifest by a wick floating in oil or by the intricate mechanism of the mighty searchlight sweeping the heavens, so truth is one and the same and varies only in the manner of its presentment to the minds and hearts of men. Always there has been a divine embodiment of truth suited to the evolution of the World at that time; and not erroneously does the Hindu religion speak of the divine incarnations guiding the cosmic changes even in pre-human Ages. To such embodiments the name of *Savior* or *Messenger* has been given by those to whom they came, and in the *name* men have seen the object of their adoration, oblivious of the oneness of the *light* they brought.

It was in this sense that the Master was the Messenger, and in this sense he was divine and human both; the Bodhisattva, the *Rassoul*, the Christ, the human vehicle bearing the light "that lighteth every man that cometh into the World"; that Spirit of Guidance which is the searchlight pouring from the bared heart of God in manifestation.

It is as the Messenger that his disciples reverence the Master most; it is the light of God shining from out his heart that they adore. And ever as that light increased, it veiled *him* more; sending its rays far out into the world, yet at its source too radiant for their human eyes to bear. For the true understanding of the Message of God, in whatever age it is brought to earth, is in the realization that it consists not in words, but in the actual *life* given to every living thing, and to every atom in the Cosmos, so long as the Messenger is in human form.

The words "I am come that ye might have *life*, and that ye might have it more abundantly,"[1] are true of each Messenger; and, as the physical sun is the source of all the life of the physical globe, so is the son of righteousness the giver of the life of the soul. The words in which that Message is given vary very little; not at all in their meaning, and in their form,

---

1 John 10:10.

44

only as the teaching given to children varies with their age and development. The Message itself is the answer to the demand of the time; and today, in the aftermath of a World destruction, the hearts of men are reaching out towards unity and peace.

"Raise us above the distinctions and differences that divide men; send us the peace of thy divine spirit, and unite us all in thy perfect being": such the prayer which the Master had ever on his lips, such the revelation of his heart towards the warring sects and religions of the World to which he came. How to write of him in this final and yet all-pervading aspect of his being? How to attempt to paint, in colours drawn from the pigments of human understanding, that life of consecration to an ever-increasing realization of his mission?

Truly was it a *Via Crucis*[2] that he trod, though it was not a visible cross that he was to bear as he passed through the jostling crowds of men, calling as of old his own in every land, and otherwise unnoticed and unknown.

The disciple who writes and another of his followers had a strange and, to their hearts, a deeply significant experience toward the close of the earthly life of the Master. Together with him they are walking in the New Forest on a still, windless day in the early

2 Way of the Cross.

autumn. As they come to one of the narrow alleys between the trees, called in the forest a *ride*, the common impulse comes to them to draw aside; and slowly the Master moves on alone. On either side of the green path the firs and pines are motionless, not a breath stirring them or the beeches and oaks that grow in the background. The Master pauses a moment, and then, turning, stands beneath a fir whose large, fan-shape branches form a canopy above his head. No wind stirs a leaf of any other tree, yet both the disciples see the branches of the fir bend and sway; slowly, and with the movement of hands in benediction, they dip towards the bared head and then become motionless as before.

After this salutation from nature, the Master resumes his slow progress along the narrow way, while the two disciples, obeying the instinct which tells them he desires to be alone, stand still to look with wonder upon a walk so kingly, and yet so fraught with the suggestion of some great compulsion and endurance, that one of them says, upon a breath of awe: "It is as if we saw him bear the cross as once before men saw it borne in royal humility before their eyes."

Three days later the two friends are sent to see the play called *The Wandering Jew* performed in London; and there in the scene which depicts the procession to Calvary, they see the cross as it is shown in the play, carried wavering and high above the crowd by a figure which is not seen. It seems to them, as they watch its slow passing, that the picture their hearts had painted has now been made complete. But for them, as for the Master, the symbol of his passing from them has been shown, although as yet they know it not.

In many ways and at all times it would seem that nature, so much beloved by him, could offer recognition and homage to the Master when human eyes were blinded by preconceived ideas and man-made theologia of the past.

On another occasion when walking with the Master in a forest the disciple saw a strange phenomenon: a small whirlwind gathers the dead leaves into a spiral form, which raises itself before him some five feet in height and three feet round at the base. At the time the forest is held in the golden stillness of October, when, if but a leaf falls, it spins slowly through the motionless air to join its fellows in the untroubled quietude of death. Yet for some three minutes the miniature vortex whirls and twists in the Master's path, as if moved by a cyclone, to subside again into the utter stillness which hushed the dreaming trees to their last sleep. Later, the disciple asks the Master what such a strange occurrence can mean, and is told "it was an initiation," yet knows that no further question must be put.

For the Messenger of God all moments may be big with portent, all places blazed, as a secret trail, with a significance unknown to those about him. The *facts* by which ordinary men make their way through the maze of human existence are to him as illusive and intangible as the changing drifts of a sea mist which obscures the outlines of the real. Nature in all her moods is open to his vision, a map whereby he guides unerringly his steps upon the way.

But most of all he reads the hearts of men and all the blotted pages of their lives; and reading, knows their failure and success, their greatness and the weakness they call *sin*. Reading, he sees how near they are to God; and as they sleep, worn out with pain and toil, he bends to smoothe the furrows on their brow and whisper dreams that bid them rise anew and tread once more the common ways of life. And as he bends above a world asleep, or partly waking in the dream of life, the light which is his being falls upon their hearts and shows in each the radiance of a star.

The Messenger of God, in every age and time, in all the worlds that strew the fields of space, in every heart that beats in human breast, has but one touch to give in passing as he goes, has but one task to render while he stays. It is to light afresh the flickering flame, to kindle once again the failing fires of that divinity within all life, that ceasing never, lifts man up to God.

Hazrat Inayat Khan was born in Baroda, India, in 1882, into a family of classical musicians. Initiated in the four major streams of Indian Sufism, he was sent to the West by his teacher, Abu Hashim Madani Chishti, "to harmonize East and West" with his music. Inayat Khan left India in 1910 and for sixteen years he lived and taught in Europe and America, bringing a message of love, harmony and beauty that was both the quintessence of Sufi teaching and a revolutionary new approach to the harmonizing of Western and Eastern spirituality. He established a school of spiritual training based upon traditional Sufi teachings infused with the vision of the unity of religious ideals and the awakening of humanity to the divinity within. Inayat Khan died in India in 1927, leaving a significant body of recorded discourse and instruction on all things pertaining to spiritual ideals in the midst of life in the world.

Sophia Saintsbury-Green

by

Suria Rebecca McBride

Murshida Sophia Saintsbury-Green

Contents

Introduction   57

First Impressions   59

Who Was She?   61

Glimpses From Her Own Words: Her Books   64
    Images of Inayat   64
    The Wings of the World   71

Glimpses from Her Own Words: Her Lectures   84
    The Path to God   87
    Human Personality   92

Editor and Poet   94

Stories Told   97

Final Years   100

Works Cited   107

Acknowledgments   109

Introduction

We find life a hard thing to understand because we identify ourselves with the form side which must break; but if we identify ourselves with the life side, as did the mystics, seers and saints, flinging away, casting to the winds, all that they possessed that they might experience that which lies beyond phenomena, this is practical mysticism, for it is the only way to understand life.

Sophia Saintsbury-Green

From time to time, certain people who play key roles in the life of others will, for one reason or another, fade from public view. In the history of universal Sufism, Sophia Saintsbury-Green appears to be one of those individuals. Her beautiful name, pleasing as it is to say and hear, is rarely spoken and may be unfamiliar even to some long-time Sufi students. But her part in furthering the Sufi Message in the West was truly significant, and she deserves to be better known.

Who was she, this Englishwoman who spent hours alongside Hazrat Inayat Khan, the Sufi master, mystic, and royal musician who brought the Sufi Message of spiritual liberty from India to the West? How did she become his traveling companion, supporting him in his work and daily life, one of the first Sufi *murshidas* (guide, senior teacher), and the first *cheraga* (minister) of the Universal Worship service? What was her contribution to Sufism through her books and lectures?

Knowing about her and the times in which she lived helps deepen our awareness of the unique atmosphere pervading the teachings and presence of Inayat Khan in Europe and the United States well before, during, and after World War I. We know that he trusted her completely. As such, she was among those chosen *mureeds* (students) who transcribed his spoken lectures for later editing and distribution.

She is most often remembered as being one of "the four murshidas" of his time, all highly intelligent women who dedicated themselves to the Sufi Message in Europe, England, and the United States—the others being Rabia Martin, Sharifa (Lucy) Goodenough, and Fazal Mai Egeling. By initiating them as murshidas, Inayat Khan was far ahead of his time in recognizing the gifts of women as spiritual leaders.[1]

---

1 In fact, only women were initiated as murshida then; he was the only murshid.

First Impressions

As a child in the 1930s, Mahmood Khan, nephew of Inayat Khan, was in her presence often during the three-month summer schools in Suresnes, France, where seekers came from many countries to learn about Sufism. He recalls that she gave a "wonderful impression." He remembers her being a "friendly, kindly, cultivated, and dignified woman—a very dear person." As a friend of the family, she was often at the dinner table; from his child's point of view he noticed the comfortable, natural relationship she had with his father, Shaikh-ul-Mashaikh (spiritual guide) Maheboob Khan.[2]

According to another first-hand account of her by a mureed attending the 1926 summer school, she was "extremely warm, almost motherly, and had an accepting personality—one felt accepted by her." In contrast to Sharifa Goodenough, who was somewhat aloof and relatively unapproachable (but an excellent editor), she was seen as very helpful to mureeds and others who might be interested in Sufism.[3]

2 Mahmood Khan, interview, February 2013.

3 Hayat Stadlinger, as related to Professor Donald (Sharif) Graham, former archivist of The Nekbakht Collection, Suresnes, and former editor-in-chief of *The Complete Works of Pir-o-Murshid Hazrat Inayat Khan.*

Theo van Hoorn, a Dutch accountant whose journal was completed by 1955, encountered her at the summer schools as well. In his *Recollections*, he calls her a remarkable figure, praising her worldly wisdom, her intense interest in widely divergent fields, her expressive personality, and her "sympathy for mureeds from all corners of the world."[4] He comments that "she approached everyone who was drawn to Murshid (Inayat Khan) and Sufism with an enthusiasm and spontaneity that gave her a special place among the Murshidas of that time."[5]

In an amusing anecdote, she is described as a "sympathetic" woman with a sense of humor. In a memoir, a young Dutch woman, Wilhemina de Koningh, wrote about her first visit to Suresnes in the 1930s:

The very first day when I arrived I was in such a heavenly mood that, seeing a very sympathetic elderly lady, I went up to her and introduced myself. I did not know that she was English and that in England a third person has to introduce you. So I got the answer: "O look, here is one introducing herself. But it is very kind of you." It was Murshida Green![6]

4 Theo van Hoorn, *Recollections of Inayat Khan and Western Sufism*, 211.
5 Ibid, 303.
6 Rani Kathleen McLaughlin and Hamida Verlinden, eds. *Pages in the Life with a Sufi*: Shahzadi Khan-de

At the time, the murshida was in her sixties—much older than the young woman in her twenties, who eventually married Musharaff Khan, Inayat Khan's youngest brother, and became a murshida with the name Shahzadi Khan-de Koningh.

Another description of Sophia Saintsbury-Green's qualities came from Angela Alt, an early mureed of Inayat Khan, who wrote of her "exquisite sensitiveness and refinement together with stoic courage; a habit of bearing misrepresentation and detraction silently; lightning quickness of perception and insight into human nature, and utter forgetfulness of self."[7]

Pir Zia Inayat-Khan, grandson of Inayat Khan, refers to her as an "erudite aristocrat."[8]

Who Was She?

Bringing Sophia Saintsbury-Green to light is not simple, however, and this partly explains why she has been so hidden from view historically. Few personal details are available, and her books reveal little about her life.

Koningh, 26.

7 Elise Guillaume-Schamhart and Munira van Voorst van Beest, eds. *Biography of Pir-o-Murshid Inayat Khan*, 510.

8 Zia Inayat-Khan, "A Hybrid Sufi Order at the Crossroads of Modernity: the Sufi Order and Sufi Movement of Pir-o-Murshid Hazrat Inayat Khan," 130.

Searching for information about her involves piecing together clues from her own writing with reminiscences from her contemporaries and descriptions by scholars and others writing about Inayat Khan.

She was born on February 27, 1866, in Southampton, England, to Elizabeth Sophia Saintsbury and Henry George Green, and was christened on April 4, 1866, at St Peter's Church in Southampton. Her given name was Emily Maud—she was to use E.M. Green or S.E.M. Green for authorship of lectures and pamphlets. But it seems that in her spiritual life she took on her mother's name, Sophia Saintsbury, and combined it with her father's name, Green. She lived in Southampton most of her life.[9]

Any other facts of her personal life come primarily from the biographical sketch by Angela Alt, which begins "Sophia Saintsbury-Green came of an old family and was reared in an atmosphere of tradition and good taste. One of her grandfathers had been High Sheriff of Berkshire; one was a boon companion of the Prince Regent and ran through three fortunes, which necessitated his son, Sophia's father, entering a profession (the first in the family to do so)." He became a solicitor,

9 According to Mahmood Khan, at 120 Gordon Avenue in Southampton and at the Lyceum Club, Piccadilly, in London.

a lawyer who gives legal advice and prepares legal documents.

She had a "vivid girlhood of study and mental attainment. She was never taught her letters but at the age of three read aloud from a page of the *Times*." That she was precocious is shown by this incident:

She was always drawn towards ancient philosophies and cultures, and at the age of five (while playing with toys upon the floor) broke into the conversation of two startled elders with her own original comment upon a two-thousand-year-old heresy which they were discussing![10]

Raised in the Anglican church, she later turned to Theosophy, as did many Europeans who were subsequently drawn to Inayat Khan. It might be said that interest in Theosophy opened a pathway to interest in Eastern religions.

Inayat Khan ordained Sophia Saintsbury-Green as the first cheraga (minister) of the Universal Worship service, a position she held for 15 months on her own; in 1921 she was designated as a *khalifa* (junior represen-tative) and in 1923 as a murshida. From 1921 to 1925, she was editor of the quarterly maga-zine *Sufism*, published in London.

---

10 Guillaume-Schamhart and van Voorst van Beest, *Biography*, 509.

Despite poor health, she dedicated herself to the exploration and furtherance of the Sufi Message throughout the rest of her life; she died on March 2, 1939.

Glimpses From Her Own Words: Her Books

Clues to Sophia Saintsbury-Green's inner life come from her two books: *Images of Inayat*, and *The Wings of the World: the Sufi Message as I See it*; two pamphlets of lectures; and unpublished addresses to cherags. She cared deeply about her subjects; her expressive writing style hints at her personality.

Images of Inayat

In her short book, *Images of Inayat*, she refers to herself only as "the disciple" or, on occasion, "the pupil." She describes experiences with Inayat Khan that reveal his essential nature— experiences such as encounters with strangers, walks on the beach of the Dutch coast, and periods of sitting with him under the shade of a tree. But while she brings forth his nature by shining the lights of language and memory, she herself is almost missing from the account.

Perhaps the closest she comes to divulging any personal information comes early in the book, in which she writes:

Pictures chase one another across the screen of memory, tears that wash the heart free of

*all but gratitude rise now after many years at
the remembrance of his graciousness and our
blindness, those of us whom as host at his own
table he served with divine humility.*

In this small paragraph, she reveals that
she is drawing on memories from years
earlier. (She refers to her little book as "these
blown leaves from memory's tree.") Omega
Publications notes the original publication
date as "about 1930." The memories come
from the time of World War I and the early
and mid-1920s. It is in those years that Inayat
Khan was traveling and lecturing extensive-
ly, initiating mureeds, holding Sufi summer
schools in France, and encouraging the growth
of the Sufi Order (and after October 1923,
Sufi Movement) in Geneva, Switzerland. Her
reference to "our blindness" speaks volumes
about the mureeds who surrounded him,
but she does not elaborate in this book. The
mention of "tears" provides a glimpse into
her grief upon learning of his sudden death in
India in February 1927 at the age of forty-four.

Instead of dwelling on her grief, however,
in *Images of Inayat* she emphasizes her gratitude for having spent time in his presence
and having witnessed the spreading of the
Sufi Message of spiritual liberty and unity.
In a passage that typifies her viewpoint, she
writes about an incident that occurred in

their travels when they had to walk some distance and then missed the tram that was to take them to his next lecture:

His serenity was unclouded through all happenings, however untoward. A picture of one such comes to the writer. It is a bitterly cold night in January, the scene a suburb in a north-country manufacturing town in England. Snow has begun to fall.... And then the waiting for a quarter of an hour in the murk and slush and bitter wind, and no word to show that the Master even felt discomfort. He spoke of different things in his even tones, and once his pupil listening had the sudden vivid impression that they stood in a cowslip meadow and that the icy wind was the soft breeze of spring.

In this passage she shows through incident and metaphor an aspect of Inayat Khan's nature and teaching. In this incident, he is shown to "do as he says" to others:

The lesson we learn from the developing of our insight is not to become excited by any influence that tries to bring us out of rhythm, but to keep in rhythm under all conditions of life; to keep our equilibrium, our tranquility under all circumstances... But at the same time, because it is difficult it is a great attainment.[11]

---

11 Hazrat Inayat Khan, Healing and the Mind World, *The Sufi Message of Hazat Inayat Khan,* vol. IV, 219.

She provides a similar example when on a cold, raw day in London, Murshid yielded his seat in a crowded train to a "poorly clad" mother and baby (while others would not), and stood the rest of the trip:

The baby taken from her and held an instant before being placed in the arms of the pupil, the mother seated in the place he had himself occupied. The low "God bless you" is spoken, and then the corridor for the rest of the journey, taken standing in its cold draught, the while his serenity and calm remain unshaken, as though he were enjoying the latest luxury of travel.

Sometimes she expresses other aspects of his nature through simple description: "As Murshid he was ever unwearied in love, patient with lack of understanding, tolerant of prejudice and ignorance, courteous toward opposition, unruffled by antagonism."

The book is a tribute composed of five sections: "The Man," "The Murshid," "The Saint," "The Master," and "The Prophet." She uses these designations as devices to highlight certain characteristics of Inayat Khan. While she clearly believes in the truth of their usage, she also explains what she means by them, which may not be the commonly understood use of the terms.

For example, in the early pages of "The Saint" section, she writes, "In those men or women to whom their fellows accord the name of Saint, the absence of that central pivotal factor of human existence, the ego or *I*, is the first and most salient appeal made to the minds of others." The result is that from the "empty reed" comes the music of Orpheus.

The music of the spheres, and the fragrance of healing balsams distilled from herbs gathered by the wayside on the road of life—such are the gifts that distinguish the Saint from other men, whether he be king or beggar, known or unknown to the world.

Here her personality in part comes through her lyrical, vivid style, which some might describe as "flowery," but others would see as reflecting her deep attunement to Inayat Khan.

Following her example, her fellow mureed, Sirkar van Stolk, later wrote about Inayat Khan in a similar vein in his book, *Memories of a Sufi Sage*: "He was an example of all those things he taught: of living in complete harmony with oneself and with one's surroundings; of being conscious of the unity underlying all forms of life."[12]

The British Sophia Saintsbury-Green and the Dutch Sirkar (born Apjar) van Stolk were both active participants in the Sufi summer

---

12 Sirkar van Stolk with Daphne Dunlop, *Memories of a Sufi Sage*, 76.

schools held in Suresnes, France, in the 1920s and 1930s. Sirkar also traveled with Inayat Khan in Europe, as well as in the United States. He was the National Representative of the Sufi Movement in Holland for 20 years; he died in 1963 while writing his book.

Beyond these simple descriptions, Murshida Green took her five categories seriously. As a former Theosophist and member of the Order of the Star, she was influenced by messianic ideas about the coming of a World Teacher or Messenger, often with Christ-like qualities. While her style may sound overblown in these passages, her true message seems to have been this: "It is as the Messenger that his disciples reverence the Master most; it is the light of God shining from out his heart that they adore."

On the other hand, Inayat Khan himself would not have identified with the five titles bestowed on him by Murshida Green. Among his closing words at the annual conference of the Sufi Order in London in July 1919, he spoke to the assembled group, saying:

I have not wanted you to revere me, or to consider me wonderful, good or great, and to raise me so high that some day you may have to throw me down from that height. I desire you to consider me friend, your brother, your comrade, someone in the world you can call in your time of need, someone who rejoices in your joy and sorrows with your sorrow.[13]

Along the same lines, his Norwegian student Bryn Beorse (given the name "Shamcher" by Inayat Khan), remembered an incident from one of the summer schools in Suresnes. One day, Murshida Green gathered together the young people there and asked them what Murshid meant to them. "So I piped up, an inspiration and a friend." But she said, "Oh you don't understand at all. He is so far above that."

That evening, before going on to deliver the evening's talk, Inayat Khan paused to mention that what he is and wants to be is "an inspiration and a friend" and that he did not like being lifted up on a pedestal. "He looked so beautifully at Murshida Green that she smiled and bowed her head."

Shamcher noted, "He always realized people's tendencies and limitations, and so he wasn't angry about what people thought. Murshida Green's talk gave him an opportunity. He always stressed that the messenger is never perfect and that this was shown in his own life."[14]

---

13 Elisabeth Keesing, *A Sufi Master Answers: On the Sufi Message of Hazrat Inayat Khan*, 20–21. Quoted from *Sufi*, January 1920, 3–4.
14 Shamcher Bryn Beorse, "Some Memories of Murshid," *The Message* Vol. 7, No. 2, February 1981, 17.

It is striking how often mureeds did describe him as their "friend," or a "fatherly friend" in an unpublished collection, "Memories of Murshid."[15] Over and over, they note his great warmth, intense humaneness, his deep, melodious voice, his sympathy and intuition, and even his "priceless sense of humor which was bound to find resonance and drive away shadows." (At the same time, in keeping with their Theosophical leanings, many of the same students also referred to him as World Teacher, Christ, and Messenger.)

The incident described by Shamcher hints at the complex relationship between Sophia Saintsbury-Green and her Murshid. According to Mahmood Khan, Inayat Khan was sometimes "a bit overwhelmed" by both her devotion and her new ideas. In addition, the dynamic of the Indian-British relationship may have been present, as she was quite British in her bearing. Despite all this, however, Inayat Khan thoroughly valued her as a wonderful, cultured person of great depth.

The Wings of the World

As is clear from reading *Images of Inayat*, Sophia Saintsbury-Green was not interested in revealing herself to the public; she originally

---

15 Shireen Smit-Kerbert, ed., "Memories of Murshid." Unpublished, known as "The Smit-Kerbert Collection."

published the book anonymously. It comes as a surprise then to see the pronoun "I" in her second book's subtitle: *The Wings of the World, or The Sufi Message As I See It*. Likewise, she began several sections in the book with the word "I."

In her thinking, the use of "I" in the subtitle has an opposite connotation to the expected one of focusing on oneself; rather, she says (in a disclaimer) that the Sufi Message in the book is seen from "one angle, that of the writer's own powers of perception and vision...." In the "Author's Note," she writes that the (sub)title in itself "precludes any suggestion of dogmatism on the part of the writer...."

The purpose of *The Wings of the World* was to present aspects of the Sufi Message, but even more interesting to us today are the descriptions of the summer schools at Suresnes, the brothers of Inayat Khan, and the beginnings of the Universal Worship service.

Summer Schools at Suresnes

What were the summer schools? Why did adults attend? What was the purpose and what were they like? As the author explains in *The Wings of the World*, the term *summer school* was given by Inayat Khan for a yearly gathering of his students in Suresnes, outside Paris, where he had settled with his family in 1922. There he lived with his wife Amina

Begum and four children[16] and his brothers in a large stone house named *Fazal Manzil* (House of Blessing) surrounded by a field and a garden.

With Inayat Khan at the center, the gatherings were held from 1922 to 1926.[17] After he died in 1927, they continued until the outbreak of World War II in 1939, under the leadership of his brother, Shaikh-ul-Mashaikh Maheboob Khan, with the support of his cousin Muhammad Ali Khan and brother Musharaff Khan. In Theo van Hoorn's *Recollections*, Sophia Saintsbury-Green is shown in the almost-annual photographs of the participants, often seated next to Maheboob Khan.

Coined by her a "school of life" for "training" in spiritual development and the "age-old practices in concentration, contemplation, and meditation," the summer schools drew students and seekers year after year.

Let us...endeavor to estimate the benefits conferred upon the personality of the man or woman who comes from the ordinary life of the world for a period of three months, or less as the case may be, to a small Sufi settlement in

---

16 His wife, who was American, was born Ora Ray Baker (1892–1949). Their four children were Noor-un-Nisa, Vilayat, Hidayat, and Khair-un-Nisa.

17 For descriptions and photographs of these gatherings, see van Hoorn, *Recollections of Inayat Khan and Western Sufism.*

the hilly suburb of Paris which is Suresnes....A very small section even of a small township, two gray stone houses, and a field, turning as the years pass into a garden...and a low hall of stone...unpretentious, yet set about with a dignified simplicity....

The life there, also simple, arranged in a quiet routine of study of the Master's teachings, papers dealing with these given by some of his followers, Meetings for Spiritual Healing and (a feature peculiar to the Sufi Movement) "Silences" of half an hour's duration, held collectively in the evening.

And so to the Summer School...come old and new members of the Movement, from Holland, from the Scandinavian countries, from Belgium, Germany, and Austria, from Italy and Switzerland, from England and America[18]...to pause awhile in the hurry of life;...to dream, to pray, to meditate, to aspire; to strip off the soiled and tattered vestures of the soul, and clothe it afresh in the white robes of purity and love.

After delving into the more spiritual aspects and practices in Suresnes, Murshida Green describes the summer school as "intensely practical": "it is a world in miniature, a working model of what will be the future of the race...a world in which national and racial

18 Also Poland and Russia. Inayat-Khan, Zia, "A Hybrid Sufi Order," 148.

distinctions have disappeared, in which the antipathies of caste and colour have been overcome...." However, ever intelligent and discerning, she acknowledges the great difficulties of attaining this vision considering the burden of ancient prejudices, barriers raised by social prestige and wealth, and such lesser considerations as personal likes and dislikes.

Sophia Saintsbury-Green was a constant presence at the summer schools. The most complete picture of her role so far comes from Theo van Hoorn's *Recollections*. It is clear that he deeply admired her, her efforts, and her books. In particular, he describes her role during the Silences in which she would shepherd each participant through the process of sitting with Murshid for a brief amount of time.

His journal's evocative description of the summer schools in the 1920s includes her:

On one of those sunny summer afternoons of 1925, just before we were to descend to the Sufi field to attend Murshid's presentation on "Architecture," I stood next to Murshida Green before the open windows of her room at the top story of the Mureeds' House. We enjoy an incomparable view of the Bois de Boulogne and of Paris behind it. On the horizon are undulations wrapped in haze that are part of the hills that surround Paris on all sides.[19]

19 van Hoorn, *Recollections*, 222

He extols the view of Paris unfolding on "this radiant afternoon" all the way to Sacre Coeur.

The Brothers

In her section on the summer schools in *The Wings of the World*, Sophia Saintsbury-Green includes eight pages describing the brothers and cousin of Inayat Khan, who were key presences during the summer schools: Maheboob Khan, Muhammad Ali Khan,[20] and Musharaff Khan. As such, she was the first author to write about their lives in India as master musicians and their passage to the West in support of their beloved Inayat Khan. "It is well here, for the benefit of the reader who is unacquainted with the (Sufi) Movement, to speak more in detail of these three, who stood so near to the Master, both by the tie of blood and by the still more binding one of devotion, reverence and great love."

In one particularly evocative passage, she writes of Maheboob Khan: "To present him to those who do not know him is to paint a portrait in pastels, so delicate are the light and shade of his nature, so subtle and fine the personality which to know is ever more deeply to appreciate." She goes on to praise the gifts

20 Even though Muhammad Ali Khan was actually a cousin, the three were known as "the brothers."

of each man, all of whom set aside their own lives to answer the call.

In fact, in a conversation about Maheboob Khan in 1933, Theo van Hoorn describes an experience introducing a Dutch mureed to those very pages in *The Wings of the World*. The mureed was not familiar with Sophia Saintsbury-Green, so Theo bought a copy of the book on the spot (in the lecture hall at Suresnes) and gave it to her. He asked her to accept it as a token of his respect for the author.

He went on to say: "And then I tell her numerous things about this remarkable figure in our Movement, who can be considered to be the Mystic of Reason, alongside Murshida Fazal Mai Egeling as Mystic of Feeling, and Murshida Goodenough as Mystic of Will."

They then looked for "a place to sit in the Sufi garden, near Murshid's tree, with a view of Fazal Manzil" and opened to the pages on Maheboob Khan, who now, as head of the Sufi Movement, was known as Shaikh-ul-Mashaikh.[21]

Beginnings of Universal Worship

Sophia Saintsbury-Green's role in the development of the Universal Worship service exemplified her relationship to Inayat Khan and the Sufi Message. She is credited with <u>helping him sha</u>pe this revolutionary, unique

21 van Hoorn, *Recollections,* 211.

way of honoring and incorporating the various religions on one altar, although she herself did not make this claim. Consistent with her humility, she does not even mention in *The Wings of the World* that she was ordained the first cheraga, continuing as the only cherag for more than a year until others were trained and had the opportunity to conduct the service.

Mahmood Khan substantiates that Sophia Saintsbury-Green "had an enormous impact on the exoteric activities, in particular the most important one, the Universal Worship." He notes that "In the 1920s when the concept of the unity of religious ideals was new in the West, the creation of the Universal Worship service was extremely important. Murshida Green was by far the most important contributor to its eventual shape." As such, he enjoys calling her "St. Paula of the Sufis."[22]

The roots of the service lay in Inayat Khan's simple Sunday prayer meetings held for his mureeds, as described by Sharifa Goodenough in London in a letter dated August 20, 1918, to Rabia Martin in California.[23] Three years

22 Mahmood Khan, interview, February 2013.
23 Graham, "Spreading the Wisdom of Sufism: The Career of Pir-o-Murshid Inayat Khan in the West," in Zia Inayat-Khan (ed.), *A Pearl in Wine: Essays on the Life, Music and Sufism of Hazrat Inayat Khan*, 142–3. See this article for more description of the early years of the Universal Worship service.

later he authorized the Universal Worship (originally called the Church of All), and Sophia Saintsbury-Green "assisted in shaping the ritual form, in which all religions are represented symbolically, to express their inner unity as well as their outer differences."[24]

Pir Zia Inayat-Khan quotes from the unpublished text "Universal Worship" in his doctoral dissertation on a hybrid Sufi order:

Pir-o-Murshid appointed Miss Dowland of Southampton, the National Representative of England, and ordained Sophia Saintsbury-Green the first Cheraga. She was the first to help Pir-o-Murshid in founding the Church of All (the Universal Worship); the religious activity of the Movement and the details of the service were thought out and settled on in Miss Dowland's sitting room (in Southampton) before the London Inaugural Ceremony which took place during a three week visit to London in May 1921.

Pir Zia goes on to comment, "This matter-of-fact description about the origination of the Church of All in tête-à-tête conversation between Inayat Khan and Sophia Saintsbury-Green in a sitting room in Southampton represents a uniquely candid account of the invention of a hybrid tradition."[25]

24 Keesing, *Biography*, 120–121.
25 Inayat-Khan, Zia, "A Hybrid Sufi Order," 129–130. See section "The Church of All" on pages 125–145 for

On May 7, 1921, the first Universal Worship service was held at the home where Shaikha Kefayat (Gladys) Lloyd lived at the time in London.[26] It was here that Sophia Saintsbury-Green was initiated as cheraga and led the service for the first time. According to a first-hand account, after the first part of the service, in which Miss Dowland read the prayers and Inayat Khan did the movements to the prayers, there was a pause when he left the room.

When he returns, he is preceded by Miss Sophia E.M. Green, who carries in her hand an unlighted candle; she walks with concentrated thoughts, towards the altar, and kneels on a cushion at Murshid's feet. Bending towards her, Murshid with his finger inscribes invisible characters upon her forehead, then sets a seal upon her forehead with the palm of his hand, lays his hands on the crown of her head, declaring her to be ordained in the Church of All, with power to illuminate herself and others. We hold our breath, realizing it is a moment of profound significance. He next lights a taper at the tall candle burning on the altar, and with this sets light to the candle which Miss Green is holding; then he helps her to rise and invests her with

a thorough discussion of the origins of the Universal Worship service and possible antecedents to the ceremony.
26 Ibid, 125.

the black silk robe of her office. Thus is the first cheraga ordained in the Church of All.

During this part of the ceremonial, feelings of love and sympathy flow out from many of the mureeds towards Miss Green, whose great honor and great responsibility they appreciate.

...The final scene consists of a recital by the cheraga, in Murshid's absence, of the prayers with the accompanying gestures. She faces the altar for the purpose, and the whole company also face the altar, the mureeds repeating the gestures in silence.

And when the little company disperses to pass into the London night, the thought in one's mind is that there has just been planted a tiny seed, which shall one day spring up into a great tree whose leaves shall be for the healing of the nation.[27]

In *The Wings of the World*, Sophia Saintsbury-Green describes the service in which candles are lit for each major religion and the scripture for each is read (accompanied sometimes by music), followed by a sermon and a blessing. She calls it a simple ceremony of dedication, sometimes called (then) the Sacrament of Light, and goes on

27 Zia Inayat-Khan, *Caravan of Souls: An Introduction to the Sufi Path of Hazrat Inayat Khan*, 175–6. See pages 173–176 for "An Account of the First Universal Worship" by Shabaz Mitchell, from the Nekbakht Foundation Archive.

to explain its significance as expressing "One God existing beneath all names and forms."[28]

As her book is intended to explain Sufi perspectives to a wider audience, she avoids terms like *cherag* (derived from the Farsi word, *chirāgh*, for light or lamp). Instead, she refers to "a priesthood of both men and women, not set apart in daily life from their fellows," who wear black, so that "the distinctions of race, creed, or caste disappear..." and their light can shine.

Regarding the black robes, Keesing explains:

Hazrat Inayat Khan would have preferred to see them officiate in light coloured robes, but to accommodate the then Western association of black with solemnity and dignity he agreed to the use of black gowns. (Sometimes he warned against too much outer solemnity and remarked that a man with a long face was not necessarily a religious man).[29]

28 In *Memories of Murshid*, Fatimah Cnoop Koopmans-Waller described the first service held at her house in Amsterdam in 1923 during which she read "wonderful texts (e.g., from the "Gayan" part of the first "Ragas")." She had been appointed as a "reader" by Murshid, who after the service said to her, "You were in ecstasy." She describes Murshida Green saying later in a talk that originally, there was to be a division of duties (one cherag to light the candles, one to conduct the ceremony, and one to deliver the sermon, plus a reader), but that was changed to the way it is done now.
29 Today, cherags wear white, gold, or brown robes.

Angela Alt states that after ordination, Murshida Green held the office "alone for fifteen months, conducting the services regularly. On becoming a *siraja*, further cherags and *sirajs* were ordained and Universal Worship spread to other countries." Originally, a siraj (derived from the Arabic word for light or lamp) was one who was appointed to guide the cherags of a particular country.

To train cherags, Inayat Khan held classes at which Murshida Green was present, and some quotes from her in the printed *Addresses to Cherags* reveal more aspects of her nature.[30] Asked by a cherag-in-training whether they should undertake a comparative study of the various religions and their scriptures, Inayat Khan turns to Murshida Green, among others, to answer. Her response reveals her sensitivity to the enormity of such a task (studying all the religions) and realism that one has limited time, and her appreciation of the importance of correctly pronouncing the sacred names in other traditions.

In another address, Inayat Khan summarizes Murshida Green's instructions: "gather your thoughts, center your mind, make your concentration on the central idea of the Universal Worship," which he defines as the Message. <u>If this happens</u>, he says, "all the inspiration

30 *Addresses to Cherags, Summer School, Suresnes 1926.*

and power will come by itself and it will flow through the cherags to the audience with that consciousness." Then obstacles will be removed and "the path will be made clear if only we each of us will maintain the consciousness of the Message."

Angela Alt expressed concisely what Universal Worship meant to Murshida Green: "The deep and esoteric side of the Message was part of her very being, but she joyed in the exoteric activity of Universal Worship; and symbolism also, as a world language appealed to her strongly, covering as it does in one sense yet suggesting and revealing to those who can see, the hidden mysteries of life."[31]

Glimpses from Her Own Words: Her Lectures

In addition to her two books, two pamphlets of lectures given by Sophia Saintsbury-Green in 1921 and 1925 provide glimpses into her nature. The lectures draw from Inayat Khan's teachings and are offered by her "with a fragrance all their own."

Angela Alt described her manner of lecturing this way:

In the later years of her mission, in order to meet the requirements of listeners who were not at home in the English language (or else

31 Guillaume-Schamhart and van Voorst van Beest, *Biography*, 509.

unfamiliar with esoteric lore) she altered her former methods and adopted a more simple and direct manner when speaking or lecturing. Perhaps in later years it was only the few who were privileged to listen when she was untrammeled by circumstances, and could freely rise and carry them to heights where momentarily under her inspiration they could view something of that heaven of wisdom which she longed to share with others.[32]

That Murshida Green was an inspiring and accomplished speaker has been confirmed by Inayat Khan's son Vilayat, who had a special relationship with her through their mutual connection to the Confraternity of the Message (see below "Final Years"). He attended one of her lectures when he was in his twenties and a student at Oxford University. Sitting and listening, he realized that one day he too would need to give public talks. Afterwards he asked her, "Your lecture was so beautiful, so polished. Every word was perfect. How on earth do you do it?" She replied, "Do you really want to know?" "Yes, please," he said. "I write it all out and then memorize it."[33] That she could do this shows both her mental strength as well as her deep intention to reach and move her listeners.

32 Ibid.
33 Donald (Sharif) Graham, interview, January 2013. As related to him by Pir Vilayat Inayat Khan.

In his journal, Theo van Hoorn remembers her lectures with great admiration. "She had a rare gift of gauging the precise reaction of her listeners to her words, so that an exchange usually ensued and Murshida Green could in turn be inspired by her audience."

He comments that while possessing a deep religious sensibility, Sophia Saintsbury-Green's "brilliant intellect" led her to investigate many aspects of modern science. "This versatility had a strong impact on her unforgettable lectures." He wrote that she "understood the art of constructing a stirring argument, based on these two pillars of faith and science, which she always managed to keep in harmonious balance...."

But even at such moments one sensed, despite the fascinating form, that her priority was to express something of the essence of what she, as a dedicated disciple of Murshid, had been able to receive from him, orally and in writing, with the intention of passing it on to anyone who was receptive. In her later years, Murshida Green displayed an almost burning desire to fulfill this ambition...."[34]

In a poignant note, which has resonance today, van Hoorn mourns the fact that her lectures were never "captured" for the future—that the "sound film and tape recorder" were

---

34 van Hoorn, *Recollections*, 303.

not available then, as they were when he was writing in the 1940s.

The Path to God

The Path to God is a compilation of four lectures given in June 1921 in London, in which Sophia Saintsbury-Green addresses the different aspects of the path to God: The Journey, The Halting Places, The Guide, and The Gate. It appears this was a series given once a week for four weeks: at the beginning of each subsequent lecture she summarizes the previous one given "last week."

Fortunately for us, in these lectures, she reveals much more of herself than in her books, perhaps because she was attempting to communicate in person to her listeners her view of life. What comes through is a learned woman with wide-ranging literary tastes who was acutely aware of her era as a time of upheaval and change for the better.

Stating her theme of life as a journey toward God, she begins with questions:

I. "The Journey." *"In all ages, among all races and peoples, one question has been asked: What is God? Who is God? Can we know God? Are we from God? Is our life in any sense a part of His Being? Do we unfold the latent power He has given us, or do we follow every wind of impulse and desire as the weathercock follows the wind?*

Noting that people have answered these questions according to their stage of evolution over the years, she remarks that "the note of oneness is the great new call to the soul today," as evidenced by the creation of the League of Nations, the new cooperation between "Capital and Labour," and the many efforts in the religious world toward unity.

"In our subject of the Path to God we shall assume that Life is the gift of God Himself: Life which holds joy and sorrow and the deepening of consciousness; it is this Life which is the Path to God." Out of this awareness, she writes joyfully:

Life now becomes a new and wonderful thing, a Quest, a Divine Adventure, a mystery, a passion; to so many life is a drab thing, because they do not realize this; life is a radiant possibility, an ever growing unfoldment; age cannot touch life lived by the soul of Man.

In Part II, "The Halting Places," she reveals her knowledge of Sufi literature, citing Jelaluddin Rumi, Hafiz, Sa'adi, Omar Khayyam, and others as putting forth this concept of life as a journey, a quest, a divine adventure.

The Sufi sees in all names and forms transitory aspects taken on by the One Life in Its progress to rejoin Its Source. In the study of Sufi literature we find that the mystics and poets laid great stress on this aspect of the journey, and have seen in different stages the resting places, the halting places, where the periods of unfoldment become definitely marked.

The halting places are those spaces in which one may stop and hear the voice of God. And, she says to her listeners, if you want to see evidence of the halting places in "this great city" of London, you need not look far. Look, she says, to Westminster Cathedral as well as the mosque, the Buddhist or Hindu temple, the synagogue, or the meeting house of the Friends (Quakers), where "...in the stillness and hush watch one after another wait till the 'still small voice' moves them, and hear the quite ordinary man or woman rise and speak words of inspiration."

In fact, this divine unrest, this quest for the soul is everywhere: "...behind the screen of matter, there are those thousands of conscious beings, young in life, ardent in spirit,... pressing for this unification of consciousness, striving to break down the barrier which divides what we call life and death."

The way she begins the next sentence shows her sensitivity to her audience when introduced to concepts that may be new and strange to them.

I do not know if I shall carry you with me when I say that to the Sufi it is not in the region of external manifestation that proof will be found, not in the séance room, nor in the consulting room of the Psycho-analyst, not in these will proof of immortality be found, but in the consciousness within, in the opening of the centres known in the East as "chakrahs," the points of contact or "chording vibrations" uniting the subtle bodies with the physical. These are the keys to open that part of the consciousness by means of which the only proof will be found.

She goes on to say the Sufi mystics knew this in the twelfth century, well before "Dante wrote his *Paradiso* and *Purgatorio*, paving the way for Suso, Eckhart, Tauler, and the other great souls who have been content to fling away with both hands all that the world holds worth while."[35]

Part III. "The Guide" begins with a quote from Inayat Khan on differences between the West and the East regarding the spiritual path. In this short lecture, Murshida Green notes that there comes a time when a guide is necessary: it is in the "condition of inner development that the Guide is sought." She describes various stages at which one might seek guidance from one who "knows not only the road of ordinary humanity, with its many Halting Places, but also the dangers and

35 Henry Suso and Johannes Tauler, fourteenth century German mystics, were students of theologian Meister Eckhart.

discoveries that lay beyond these in the desert and the uncharted lands." She advises caution against "false guides" and stresses that "the true Guide is never absent when the soul asks for his presence; but the *soul* must seek."

Some people are afraid of the term Master, *but if they are not willing to acknowledge a Master they can never become a Servant; and to become the Servant of God is to fulfill the purpose of life. Life today is in flux, change is all around us, but of one thing be sure, it cannot turn back, it will go forward to new unfoldment of its inherent divinity. And we, if we would go onward, must seek the Guide who will lead us from the known to the unknown. The soul, in its quest for God, should welcome all that comes to him as a new experience, for while newness can rise in a life as the dawn, the life that is lived is the life of the inner man whom age cannot touch nor any death defile.*

She begins Part IV. "The Gate" this way: "We have chosen to use this word rather than that which is more usually taken to express the conception of human progress known as Initiation, namely the Goal, because it is not only less hackneyed but also more picturesque in its connotation." It soon becomes clear that she is using the word "initiation" to refer to stages in spiritual and human development and not, as used in Sufi orders today, to indicate *Bayat* (stages of initiation of mureeds).

In this longer lecture she discusses seven gates of initiation as inner processes of awakening consciousness throughout one's life, beginning with the first gate, human birth.

According to this view life itself is the great initiator; this physical life in which we possess a body containing centres which when properly developed present life as an ordered series of openings of consciousness. Sufi Mystic Philosophy lays the greatest possible stress on the value of human life; it does not regard it in any of its aspects as the result of a "Fall," nor does it teach that the "redemption of the body" is anything other than the gradual process of the permeation of matter by spirit which is the true at-one-ment.

She ends her description at the fifth gate, which is the "birth of the spiritual life of the soul" and concedes that perhaps another series of lectures might "enlarge on this most wonderful of all themes."

Human Personality

The pamphlet *Human Personality* is a compilation of three lectures on life published in 1925. As such, they are both lyrical and practical, addressing the meaning of life with three themes: The Music of Life, The Passion of Life, and The Ashes of Life, given in sequence, each building on the other. Consistent with her unassuming personality, she herself notes that she would rather call them "Addresses" or "Talks," as she very much dislikes the word *lecture*. And she stresses that she does not dogmatize, but rather offers thoughts as to the purpose of life.

In her first talk, drawing most likely on Inayat Khan's *The Mysticism of Sound*, she has as her theme the "rhythm of life—rhythm or vibration—is at the back of all manifestation. ...each atom, and each individual made up of atoms, has its own note, its own rhythm, its own particular vibration; and to strike that sound, to find that rhythm perfectly, is to live life perfectly and fully."

Later, in the third talk, she comes to the great process of life: "every moment has its beginning and its ending, and every moment throws out its essence and leaves its ashes." The fermentation process of experience, the burdens of the mental body, the clearing away to the essence, and the understanding of others' circumstances are all themes she brings forth to her listeners—ending with a hope for a new consciousness, a New Age.[36]

For, as she says, contrary to the thought that mysticism is not practical, "To me, it is

---

36 Most likely she heard this term used by Theosophist Helena Blavatsky.

the only thing that is practical, because in everything that we see around us the mystic looks for what it (life) is producing." Speaking between the two world wars, she says:

The things that you and I knew, the sanctities of life, all the things that we thought we were so sure and safe, the things that we could rely on, there is not one single thing that you can name that remains the same, as it did fifteen or twenty years ago. The relations of parents and children, of husband and wife, of men and women not related to each other, of young people, all these things are making themselves anew. And we must believe that the Great Alchemist knows what He is doing.

What is our duty? For that is the practical result of all this thought. Our duty must surely be to see to it that we do not hinder by keeping the ashes that have to be removed; that we liberate ourselves, as far as possible, from prejudices and from old ways of thinking, and from the dead matter that clogs freedom of expression, believing that God is Life....

Editor and Poet

In addition to being a writer of prose, Sophia Saintsbury-Green was an editor. In her editorial in the first issue of *Sufism* in May 1921, under the name Sophia E.M. Green, she wrote:

With the present issue the little Quarterly Sufism *makes its first appearance in the world of letters as successor to* The Sufi.... *Its message is to the heart which is the "abode of God" from the point of view of Sufi mysticism: the heart which in all humanity is closed and silent as an empty temple until Love, which is God, takes up His dwelling there. When human love touches the life of the individual we see the awakened heart: but when Divine Love enters, the winged heart soars upward as the lark to the sun.*

And then on a practical note:

In the first-hand Teachings of Pir-o-Murshid which will appear in the quarterly edition of Sufism *those who desire to see life and its problems with the eyes of the heart will have an opportunity of doing so: they will also gain information as to all meetings and classes which will be held in London and be kept in touch with the work of the Sufi Order.*

Following this editorial are news items on the visits of Inayat Khan to Switzerland and Holland, where he formed his first circle of Dutch pupils. It is reported that he enjoyed the naturalness of character and hospitality of the Dutch people.

It appears that 1921 was an important year for beginnings. *The Bowl of Saki* sayings were most likely collected by Sophia Saintsbury-Green for its first printing in 1921. As editor of *Sufism*, she requested that Pir-o-Murshid "add a few words asking all your mureeds to get a copy (of *The Bowl of Saki*) and read it daily so that we may all be united in the same thought all over the world."[37]

As editor, presumably she was free to include poetry of her own in the magazine. In the March 1923 issue, she wrote a long poem entitled "The Christ," which is a dialogue between Jesus and Satan. In December 1923, she published *Three Poems* under the name Murshida S.E.M. Green: "Fana-Fi-Sheikh—Devotion to the Master"; "Fana-Fi-Rasoul—Devotion to the Christ"; and "Fana-Fi-Allah—Annihilation in the Divine." In the December 1924 issue, she included a poem dating from 1909 on "The Redemption of the Body," which alternates stanzas headed by *The Soul Speaks* and *The Soul Listens*.

Her name is also indicated as having input, most likely as an editor, regarding the wording of the *Gayatri*, specifically the prayers Saum and Salat.[38] It makes sense that since these prayers became part of the Universal Worship service, she would have contributed some editorial changes. It appears we can thank

37 Conveyed in a letter by Miss Nargis Dowland to Hazrat Inayat Khan. *Complete Works of Pir-o-Murshid Hazrat Inayat Khan, Original Texts: Sayings, Part II.*
38 *Complete Works of Pir-o-Murshid Hazrat Inayat Khan, Original Texts: Sayings, Part I*, 200–201, 203.

her for "Take us in thy Parental Arms" among other wordings.

Stories Told

As with any leader or public figure, certain stories by and about Sophia Saintsbury-Green have been handed down by those who have studied this remarkable era of the Sufi Message in the West.

The first, told by her in *Images of Inayat*, concerns a kind of telepathic transfer of knowledge that occurred on a train trip through the "devastated areas" between Paris and Holland after World War I. She describes at great length the experience of sitting next to Inayat Khan when he closes the compartment door so that the two of them are alone and able to concentrate fully. Shakti Monnevan Stolk, sister of Sirkar van Stolk, gives a simpler description in *Memories of Murshid*:

Murshida Green has also told us how she traveled by train through Belgium with Murshid, and she asked him what a battlefield in the last war must have looked like. Murshid then conjured up the condition of a battlefield before her mind's eye. She saw everything. She saw how huge white apparitions carried the dead with them and nursed the wounded.

In another story in *The Wings of the World*, Murshida Green evokes a foretelling by Inayat Khan of the vision of the Sufi Message alive in

the world. In 1925, seven years after the signing
of the Armistice after World War I:

*...the Master was again sitting by the waters
of the Lake (Geneva) with one of his disciples
(herself). "How strange," said the latter, "how
strange, Murshid, that you should have chosen
Geneva for the International Headquarters of
the Sufi Movement, and that the same place
should have been selected by the League of
Nations." The Master turned with a smile. "Is
it so strange?" he said. "Perhaps the same place
was chosen for these two activities at the same
time and by the same thought! When I was here
in the spring of 1914—I have seen them both as
they would be later, after the War." Then the
disciple understood that both were manifesta-
tions of the Message of the Day.*

A third story has been shared in Sufi circles
over the years for both its dramatic quality
and its important outcome—the vision and
ultimate establishment of Murad Hassil, the
Sufi temple built at Katwijk-aan-Zee in The
Netherlands. Sophia Saintsbury-Green first
told the story in her chapter on "The Prophet"
in *Images of Inayat*.

Pir Zia Inayat-Khan introduces the story
this way: "During the Dutch Summer School
(two weeks in September 1922) an incident
occurred that was to quickly find its way into
the (Sufi) Order's most prized hagiographical

traditions. Sophia Saintsbury-Green provides an eloquent eyewitness account."[39]

In her account, she starts out slowly:

The scene: a little village on the coast of Holland, then but a collection of fishermen's huts at one end of the beach, and at the other a few hotels, open for summer visitors, but at that season closed and silent.

She goes on to describe the unusual behavior of Murshid at breakfast at the home of their host, Sirdar van Tuyll. He seemed restless and quiet that morning, and after lunch asked her and Sirdar to accompany him for a walk by the dunes. They set out together, but soon Murshid asked the two to wait while he went on alone. She describes him as walking uncharacteristically quickly, and with head uncovered: "his hair, usually so expressive of his love of beauty, is all disheveled and streams out upon the wind." To her, he looked like a prophet with his long black cassock and overcoat.

After about three-quarters of an hour, they saw him return with his usual calm and measured gait. Stooping to gather "flowers, the wild and hardy poppies of the sea, the thistle and the yellow spikes of gorse," "he smiles the heavenly smile that wins their hearts, and, bending, lays the flowers in his pupil's hands."

---

39 Inayat-Khan, Zia, "A Hybrid Sufi Order," 149–151.

Only later in the day did he speak of the incident. He asked Sirdar if he can find the spot, "a tiny basin green and fresh with grass," that he had come upon when disappearing from view. He said, "For from today, it shall be given the name Murad Hassil, the Mount of Blessing, and those who pray for blessings there shall have their wish granted."

It is here that the Universel Murad Hassil was built in 1969.

Final Years

After the sudden death of Inayat Khan on February 5, 1927, Sophia Saintsbury-Green must have felt the loss of her Murshid deeply, as did so many mureeds who did not know he was in India at the time. It is clear, however, that she continued to carry on the work of spreading the Sufi Message through various means, such as her books, her lectures, her leading of the Universal Worship service, and her involvement in two new spheres: Zira'at and the Confraternity of the Message.[40]

The Zira'at concentration, which uses the symbols and processes of agriculture as ways to bridge the spiritual and material worlds, was in the planning stages with her help shortly before Inayat Khan died. Evidence of this is shown in the transcript of her address to the Jamiat Am at the International Headquarters

40 Ibid, 142.

of the Sufi Movement in Geneva, Switzerland, on June 15, 1930.[41]

In her remarks, she described a conversation she had with Inayat Khan during the 1926 summer school.

...when I went into his presence and asked, "Murshid, will you tell me something about the ceremony I am interested in, Zirat?" and he replied: "We will talk about the Confraternity of the Message." And I laid aside my little book, with the notes of Zirat, and took out the book I now have with the short jottings.

On September 13, 1926, along with the ceremony of laying the foundation stone for a Sufi temple (the Universel),[42] Inayat Khan also instituted the Confraternity of the Message. The purpose of this activity was to spiritually build the temple by means of prayer (a set of Sufi prayers recited for morning, mid-day, and evening).[43] On that day, he initiated his son, Vilayat, then ten years old, as head—and Murshida Green as Warden until Vilayat came of age—of the Confraternity. He received an initial twenty-five mureeds into the Confraternity at this the last summer school of his life.

41 Provided by Mahmood Khan, October 2013.

42 As depicted in the documentary film, *Memories of a Mystic: An Intimate Portrait of Pir Vilayat Inayat Khan*, Sacred Spirit Music, 2004. Sophia Saintsbury-Green is seen in the film.

43 Inayat-Khan, Zia. "A Hybrid Sufi Order," 189.

In the same 1930 address cited above, Murshida Green described the intense preparation for the ceremony. Adamantly refuting the notion that the Confraternity of the Message was her idea (which apparently many mureeds felt), she recounted Inayat Khan's interest in the ceremony and his involvement, down to every detail:

During more than two-thirds of the time (at the 1926 summer school), every Sunday morning of his most valuable time was devoted to a careful, meticulously accurate consideration of the ceremony which was his last and crowning act among us…. And he thought out every single paragraph of that very intricate ceremony; everything that was to be carried by each person was his thought, the thought of the Messenger, who is not concerned with these little things.[44]

As is clear from the photographs taken at Suresnes, Murshida Green continued attending the summer schools throughout the 1930s until her death in 1939.

To summarize the life of Sophia Saintsbury-Green, it seems fitting to quote from Pir-o-Murshid Hazrat Inayat Khan himself. From his *Autobiography* are these words:

---

44 A rare sarcastic note on her part, meaning that mureeds seemed to feel he would not be concerned with ceremonial details but rather would delegate them to her or even allow her to design them.

Miss Green (Sophia), who was a Theosophist for most of her life, a special pupil of Mrs. Besant[45] and who through Theosophy came to recognize the Truth sent in the Sufi Message, was made a Khalifa in England, and then was promoted to be a Murshida, who during my absence watered the plant which I had sown in the soil of England, proving thereby worthy of the work entrusted to her. The inspiration and efficiency she has shown in presenting the Message to her people, her sagely character, with her receptivity to the Message, has been of great importance to the Cause. Her assistance in bringing out my works has been of immense value.

She has been the first to help me in founding the Church of All, the religious activity, which was introduced in England by her. She was ordained the first Cheraga, and carried out the work most satisfactorily. She edited the magazine Sufism, *which has succeeded the periodical called* The Sufi, *which had come out before. Her booklet, lately published, is called* The Path to God. *She wrote a pamphlet called* Human Personality.[46]

It is clear from this description that Inayat Khan placed a deep trust in the devoted

---

45 Annie Besant, Theosophist and cofounder of the Order of the Star.

46 Guillaume-Schamhart and van Voorst van Beest, *Biography*, 149, 152

Murshida Green, honoring her qualities of inspiration, receptivity, practicality, and wisdom. Initiating her as a murshida and the first cheraga for the Universal Worship service, he gave her great scope for her creativity and her ability to express the inner meaning of the Message.

In his support of her and the other murshidas, Inayat Khan showed his recognition of the importance of women in spiritual leadership during a time when most churches relegated women to traditional altar guild and service roles. He said:

There is no line of work or study which woman in the West does not undertake and does not accomplish as well as man. Even in social and political activities, in religion, in spiritual ideas, she indeed excels man. The charitable organizations existing in different parts of the West, are mostly supported by women, and I see as clear as daylight that the hour is coming when woman will lead humanity to a higher evolution.[47]

Roots of his advanced attitude may be found in his childhood and years of growing up in a family that honored women. The influence of "the ladies of the house" was strong and long-lasting. His brother, Musharaff Khan, recalls his own experience as a child being

47 Ibid, 242–243.

taken for guidance to a murshida, "a holy lady, whose power you felt at once in the peace of her presence."[48]

Returning to the topic of her melodious name, perhaps the words of Murshid Samuel L. Lewis (Sufi Ahmed Murad Chisti), can shed some light. In his essay on "The Place of Womankind in the New Age," he wrote these words:

Practice brings awakening. Centering in the heart means the arousal of the heart functions. Thus love, thus tenderness, thus insight, thus the Sophia, which is the deification of feminine wisdom....In this way there will be a return and an increase of wisdom (Sophia) and womankind may fulfill itself in higher social, psychic, occult and mystical aspects of life. Her guidance may then be sought by the whole of humanity.[49]

Viewed in this way, the name "Sophia" is absolutely right for this woman who became murshida, writer, editor, lecturer, and shaper of containers to support the Sufi Message of spiritual liberty. Theo van Hoorn notices this connection as well: "I can talk almost forever about Murshida Green; about her deep

---

48 Musharaff Khan, *Pages in the Life of a Sufi: Reflections and Reminiscences of Musharaff Moulamia Khan*, 37–38.

49 Samuel L. Lewis, *Toward Spiritual Brotherhood*, 48.

wordly wisdom, already suggested by her first name, 'Sophia'...."[50]

Sophia Saintsbury-Green continues to be something of a mystery, and we can be sure she would have preferred to remain unknown. We are drawn to her despite her wishes, however. As waterer of the plant of the Sufi Message during its time of seeding, growing, and flourishing in the West, she warrants the attention and gratitude of those of us who came later.

---

50 van Hoorn, *Recollections*, 211.

Works Cited

Beorse, Shamcher Bryn. "Some Memories of Murshid," *The Message* Vol. 7, No. 2, February 1981, 14–18. New Lebanon: Sufi Order International.

Graham, Donald A. Sharif. "Spreading the Wisdom of Sufism: The Career of Pir-o-Murshid Inayat Khan in the West," in *A Pearl in Wine: Essays on the Life, Music and Sufism of Hazrat Inayat Khan*. Zia Inayat-Khan ed. New Lebanon: Omega Publications, 2001.

Guillaume-Schamhart, Elise, and Munira van Voorst van Beest, eds. *Biography of Pir-o-Murshid Inayat Khan*. Suresnes, France: Nekbakht Foundation; London and The Hague: East-West Publications, 1979.

Inayat Khan, Hazrat. *Addresses to Cherags, Summer School, Suresnes 1926*. Sarasota: Rising Tide International Edition, 2004.

———*The Complete Works of Pir-o-Murshid Hazrat Inayat Khan, Original Texts: Sayings, Part I*. Munira van Voorst van Beest ed. London and The Hague: East-West Publications, 1982, 1989.

———*The Complete Works of Pir-o-Murshid Hazrat Inayat Khan, Original Texts: Sayings, Part II*. Munira van Voorst van Beest ed. London and The Hague: East-West Publications, 1990.

———*Healing and the Mind World, The Sufi Message of Hazat Inayat Khan, Vol. IV*. Geneva: International Headquarters Sufi Movement, 1961, 1982.

Inayat-Khan, Zia. "A Hybrid Sufi Order at the Crossroads of Modernity: the Sufi Order and Sufi Movement of Pir-o-Murshid Hazrat Inayat Khan." PhD diss. Duke University, 2006.

———*Caravan of Souls: An Introduction to the Sufi Path of Hazrat Inayat Khan.* New Lebanon: Omega Publications, Sulūk Press, 2013.

Keesing, Elisabeth. *A Sufi Master Answers: On the Sufi Message of Hazrat Inayat Khan.* London: Fine Books, Ltd.; The Hague: East-West Publications; Delhi: Motilal Banarsidass, 1997.

Khan, Musharaff Moulamia. *Pages in the Life of a Sufi: Reflections and Reminiscences of Musharaff Moulamia Khan.* Wassenaar: Mirananda Publishers, 1982.

Lewis, Samuel L. *Toward Spiritual Brotherhood.* Sufi Ruhaniat International, 1978.

McLaughlin, Rani Kathleen, and Hamida Verlinden, eds. *Pages in the Life with a Sufi: Shahzadi Khan de Koningh.* Stichting Soefi Museum Pir-O-Murshid Musharaff Khan, http://www.sufimovement.org, 2012.

Saintsbury-Green, Sophia E.M. *Human Personality: Three Lectures.* Southampton: Camelot Press, 1925.

———*Images of Inayat.* New Lebanon: Omega Publications, 1992. Originally published anonymously as *Memories of Hazrat Inayat Khan by A Disciple.* London: Rider & Co., n.d. (c. 1930).

———*The Path to God: Verbatim notes of a series of Lectures given in June, 1921.* Southampton:

Book Depot for Sufi Literature, 1922.

——*The Wings of the World or The Sufi Message As I See It.* Deventer: A.E. Kluwer; London: Luzac & Co., n.d. (c. 1934).

Smit-Kerbert, Shireen, ed., "Memories of Murshid." Seattle: Sufi Order; Fazal Manzil Archive, n.d. Unpublished.

van Hoorn, Theo. *Recollections of Inayat Khan and Western Sufism.* Translated, annotated and introduced by Hendrik J. Horn. Leiden: Foleor Publishers, 2010.

van Stolk, Sirkar, with Daphne Dunlop. *Memories of a Sufi Sage.* The Hague: East-West Publications Fonds B.V, 1967.

Acknowledgments

Although Sophia Saintsbury-Green may be unknown to many, she is beloved by those who are drawn to the history of Sufism and Hazrat Inayat Khan. In researching her Sufi life, I was continually surprised and gratified by the enthusiasm of these dedicated souls and by their desire to speak about her and her gifts.

The first person I contacted was, naturally, Donald (Sharif) Graham, former archivist, The Nekbakht Foundation. His welcoming attitude and generous contribution of information helped launch me on this project. Without his joyful response, I would not have been able to undertake the work, and for all of that I give thanks. He also pointed me to the current archivist, Qahira A.L. Wirgman, who unhesitatingly provided copies of the precious lectures written by Murshida Green.

Shaikh-ul-Mashaikh Mahmood Khan has been a constant guide who gave freely of his time, attention, and energy to both the remembrance of the times and the writing of this profile. As a child growing up in the presence of Sophia Saintsbury-Green, he remembers her with affection and respect. I am deeply grateful to him and feel privileged to have benefited from his own pleasure in re-calling those early years.

I thank my teacher Khadija Julia Goforth for her open-hearted support and sensitive, thorough review of the draft. My soul sisters in research were Nizam Ellen Ash and Fateah Alice Saunders. Wahhab Sheets, secretary general of the Sufi Order International, and Suhrawardi Gebel, who formerly held that position, gave steady support and guidance. Hamida Verlinden, secretary, International Headquarters of the Sufi Movement, supplied photographs of Murshida Green.

My heartfelt appreciation goes to Pir Zia Inayat-Khan, Sufi Order International, and Pir Shabda Kahn, Sufi Ruhaniat International, for their ongoing encouragement.

Suria Rebecca McBride

Suria Rebecca McBride is a freelance writer and editor. She earned her PhD. in English from the University of Pennsylvania and her B.A. in English from Oberlin College. Author of *Traveling Between the Lines: Europe in 1938*, she lives with her husband in Old Chatham, New York.

*For more information on
Hazrat Inayat Khan and Sufism
please contact:*

Inayati Order
112 East Cary Street
Richmond VA 23219
www.inayatiorder.org

www.ingramcontent.com/pod-product-compliance
Lightning Source LLC
Chambersburg PA
CBHW031859090426
42741CB00005B/567